How Green Is Your Class?

Also available from Continuum

100 Ideas for Teaching Citizenship, Ian Davies

100 Ideas for Teaching Geography, Andy Leeder

Bringing the World into the Primary Classroom, Tony Pickford

How Green Is Your Class?

Over 50 Ways Your Students Can Make a Difference

KATE BROWN

continuum

Continuum International Publishing Group
The Tower Building, 11 York Road, London, SE1 7NX
80 Maiden Lane, Suite 704, New York, NY 10038

www.continuumbooks.com

British Library Cataloguing-in-Publication Data
A catalogue record for this book is available from the British Library.

ISBN: 9781847061225 (paperback)

Library of Congress Cataloguing-in-Publication Data
The Publisher has applied for CIP data.

Typeset by Newgen Imaging Systems Pvt Ltd, Chennai, India
Printed and bound in Great Britain by MPG Books, Cornwall

To my parents

Contents

Acknowledgements

I would like to thank Peter Pattisson, National Subject Lead at the Association for Citizenship Teaching, and Peter Hayes, Director of CSV Education, for their comments on the manuscript. I would also like to thank form 8.1 for volunteering their work and for their enthusiasm for changing the world.

1 | About this book

Young people can make a difference

Young people, like adults, are faced daily with small and huge injustices: at home, at school, in their local communities, on the news. Their capacity for outrage and their heightened sense of social justice mean they can be quick to identify the need for change. How often do you hear students say 'Miss, that's not fair', or 'Miss, how can I make a difference'?

Like adults, young people have voices that can be used to bring about the change they think is needed. They may not be able to vote and have limited spending power, but they have resources of time, creativity and persuasion. From the small decisions they make everyday to the career they choose, young people's actions have an impact, and they can use them to make a difference. Increasingly, channels are being constructed for this power for change, as organizations and institutions recognize young people's right to express their views on issues that affect them.

While this right may be enshrined in the United Nations Convention on the Rights of the Child, it cannot be assumed that young people will know how to use their 'voice'. They are unlikely to enter adult life as active citizens if they have not had the opportunity to develop the skills they need to participate effectively. Only through being active themselves, having the chance to really make a difference, can they develop their sense of agency.

However, it is not always clear to students, or their teachers, where such opportunities for action lie. Schools can be confusingly participatory and autocratic by turn, students are too young for the more obvious forms of democratic participation, and local government can seem both baffling and boring.

This book identifies opportunities for real student activism. It is a guide for teachers on how to support their students to make a difference. Over 50 actions are outlined, all with the potential to bring about change: at home, school, locally, nationally and internationally, on any issue that young people choose.

These 'change actions', can be used flexibly by teachers: with classes or smaller groups; in school time or for homework; as one-off practical activities or term-long campaigning projects; to stretch able and focused students and to motivate disengaged young people. Above all, they are intended to be used to inspire and equip young people to make a difference now and in the future.

What is in this book?

This book is divided into five main sections (Chapters 2–6), each tackling a different type of change action.

There are some issues for which students directly hold the power to make a change. By making small, everyday adjustments to the way they live their lives they can make a difference to the planet and human welfare. These everyday, practical actions are the focus of Chapter 2.

On many issues, students do not directly hold the power to bring about change. Instead they will need to influence those who do. Chapter 3 details strategies for raising awareness, and Chapter 4 identifies ways of putting pressure on those in power. Students can also get themselves elected or selected to a position that holds more decision-making power; this is the subject of Chapter 5. Finally, for ideas on what and how students can donate, see Chapter 6.

Each of these chapters contains a number of activities, or change actions, through which young people can bring about change. The information in each section is intended to help teachers guide their students to consider the relative merits of the different change actions, and to select the most appropriate and effective. It is likely that much of this material will not be entirely new to many teachers. It is included here so that teachers do not have to spend their time looking up additional information and making it accessible for students.

Suggestions on how to get students thinking about the underlying issues, and how to support their actions, are also included.

If you or your students do want to know more, there are recommended sources in the 'Find out more' sections, along with the web addresses of organizations through which young people can take action. Information on the web changes quickly; if you find that a web address quoted is no longer accurate, try searching for an up-to-date site using the name of the organization. There are further, more general, useful resources listed in Chapter 7.

In some places, additional explanations that are not themselves actions for change are included. This background information, found in 'boxes' in the text, is directed at a universal 'you'. These are intended either as a quick reminder of the key issues for teachers, or to be copied and given directly to students to help them understand concepts they may not be familiar with.

How can I use this book?

There are two main ways in which teachers can use the actions in this book to support their students to make a difference.

First, change actions can be approached through a topic of study, by incorporating real opportunities for involvement in existing schemes of work and lesson plans. Alternatively, students can be challenged to consider what they would like to see changed about the world. By researching, selecting, planning and carrying out a change action, students will learn more about the underlying issues.

Some of the change actions in this book can be achieved entirely in the classroom (e.g. writing an email, designing a poster). Other actions, such as buying fairtrade products or getting elected to the student council, have to be completed out of lesson time. Either way, teachers can help students to consider their options and plan their actions in class, and give them opportunities to report back on what they have achieved. This support can be adapted to suit the context and time available: teachers can use an action-pledge as a quick plenary, or take students through the steps to mount a full-scale campaign.

Incorporate change actions into Citizenship lessons

Citizenship provides a specific, and mandatory, window for teaching students how to make a difference. The subject specifically aims to equip students with the knowledge and skills they need to take action and make a difference in their communities and the wider world.

Not only that, but the new curriculum, which will be implemented in schools from September 2008, states directly that the knowledge and understanding of Citizenship should be developed while using and applying Citizenship skills. In other words, all Citizenship teaching should include opportunities to develop skills of critical thinking and enquiry, advocacy and representation and informed and responsible action.

Incorporating the change actions in this book into Citizenship schemes of work, whether taught in discrete lessons or across the curriculum, can provide such opportunities. The change actions can be used as part of the teaching and learning on the full range of Citizenship topics, including: political, legal and human rights; young people and the law; local and national government and elections; different forms of government beyond the UK; public services and the voluntary sector; information and the media; the economy; consumer and employee rights; the UK's diverse society; migration; conflict resolution; sustainable development; European and global communities and the challenges they face. The change actions also directly address the element of the curriculum which requires students to learn about the actions that individuals, groups and organizations can take to influence decisions affecting communities and the environment. The 'More useful resources' section in Chapter 7 contains links to teaching materials on some of these strands.

Some change actions will be more appropriate in certain contexts, but on almost any topic there is an email petition students can sign, online forums they can contribute to, someone they can write to, awareness to be raised or relevant charities they can donate to. Here are just a few examples of the ways in which change actions can be incorporated into Citizenship lessons:

◆ As part of a unit on local government, support students to email their local councillor with a problem they have identified in the local community, or a compliment on how local affairs are run. Help students find out the name and contact details of their representatives, and guide them on how to put together a good letter or email. Even better, local councillors could be invited to the school so that students can speak to them directly.

◆ As part of a unit on migration, ask students to find out as much as they can about what it might be like to be an asylum seeker arriving in the UK. For what reasons do people leave their home country? What situation do they face if they make it to the UK? Show them how they can use this information to write an article for the school magazine, prepare an assembly or make a display, to make other students more aware of the problems refugees face.

◆ As part of a unit on human rights, ask students to identify human rights violations in their lives or in the news. Support them to take action against these, for example, through using Amnesty International's letter writing campaign, or educating their peers about their rights.

♦ As part of a unit on the role of the voluntary sector, allow time for students to research the work of a specific charity. What does the charity do? Do they think it has a positive impact? Why? For a charity they have chosen, help them to formulate a strategy to make a donation. Provide planning time in class, and talk students through how they can increase awareness of their fundraising event.

♦ As part of a unit on the changing nature of UK society, encourage students to research on the internet or talk to their peers about different ways of being or beliefs. Challenge them to tell someone else what they have learnt, in person or via the internet, using email, 'blogs', or even 'podcasts'.

♦ As part of a unit on the global community, encourage students to consider their links with people and organizations in other parts of the world. How can what they buy affect people in far away places? How can they use their consumer power to make a difference to these people's lives? Can they script a conversation they could have with their parents to encourage them to buy a fairtrade product, or email, write to or boycott a company whose ethical practice they are concerned about?

Using change actions like these in lessons helps teachers meet the Citizenship curriculum requirements for learning opportunities. These include: working individually and in groups; participating in school-based and community-based activities; participating in different forms of individual and collective action (including decision making and campaigning); taking into account a range of contexts (school, local, regional, national, European, international and global); and using and interpreting different media and technologies both as sources of information and as a means of communicating ideas.

Not every action that makes a difference develops skills of Citizenship. Practical actions where students help an individual (such as resolving a conflict between friends) are often seen as relevant to students' learning about their relationships with others, rather than their role in public life. In addition, where young people take part in change actions that bring about change in their community, but without any understanding of or involvement in planning the action, they do not necessarily develop their skills of participation.

Examples include photocopying or envelope stuffing for an organization, or holding a collection tin at the end of an assembly.

Certainly, 'token' Citizenship activities where students complete an action which has been planned for them, and do not reflect on what they did, are unlikely to develop the knowledge and skills students need to take action and make a difference. However, most actions can contribute to students becoming informed, critical, active citizens if the process is focused on as much as the action itself. That means ensuring that students are developing their Citizenship skills, laid out in the Citizenship curriculum, as they complete the change action.

By researching, planning and undertaking enquiries into issues and problems, interpreting and critically analysing sources, and questioning and reflecting on different viewpoints, students develop the Citizenship skills of critical thinking and enquiry. In learning how to explain their own viewpoint, as well as opposing views, and persuading others to think again, they learn skills of advocacy and representation. Skills of informed and responsible action are developed by exploring creative approaches to taking action on a problem, and researching, initiating, planning and analysing the impact of an action.

If young people are encouraged to research and evaluate underlying problems, if they take part in decisions on what can be done and how, and if they reflect on the progress they have made, personally and for their communities, they can learn as active citizens. This process is explored further in this chapter, in the section 'Challenge students to take a change action of their choice'.

Incorporate change actions into other subject lessons

The actions in this book are not only relevant to teaching and learning Citizenship, but they can also be used in other subjects too. Indeed, the Citizenship curriculum states that students should have the opportunity to make links between Citizenship and work in other subjects and areas of the curriculum. The following are just a few examples.

In Geography, students must explore the idea of global Citizenship. While teaching about sustainable tourism, ask students to research and put together a pack for their peers and families on ways to reduce the environmental and social impact of their holiday. As part of a unit on the use of resources, set students the task of writing a proposal for the school council for a paper-recycling scheme, or to research and keep a diary of the energy savings they can make in a week.

In English, students learn how to prepare to speak in formal situations, and how to compose persuasive writing (in forms such as advertisements, articles and letters). These are great opportunities for students to research issues of particular concern to them. Providing a 'real' context, in which they actually deliver the speech to a relevant audience or have the article published, completes a change action and is extremely motivating.

This is also true of many of the skills developed in Information and Communication Technology (ICT). For example, searching for, and questioning, information on a specific issue; using technology, including email, to share and exchange information effectively; and using ICT to create presentations. By sending a lobbying email, or raising awareness through researching and creating a presentation on a topical or local issue, students can develop ICT and Citizenship skills together.

A final example is that teachers involved in careers advice can encourage students to consider the power for change they will have in different careers.

Challenge students to take a change action of their choice

As well as approaching change actions through existing curriculum topics, the change actions in this book can be used to approach a topic. Challenge students to identity a problem or issue that they would like to see changed. By researching, selecting, planning and carrying out an action, students will learn more about the underlying issues. This approach could be used in Citizenship, form-time or Personal, Social and Health Education (PSHE); in lesson time over a few weeks or as an activity for a collapsed timetable session. Disengaged students can find motivating the freedom to make choices about the issue they want to see changed and the change action they want to take. With sufficient support they can develop their skills and their sense of achievement.

Teachers will need to guide their class or group through a number of steps. First, individually or in groups, students need to explore what they think needs changing. What do they hate enough to make a difference? What do they see that they think is unjust: at school, in their local communities, nationally or internationally? It is important that students feel a sense of ownership over their choice of issue, but it can also be practically helpful to limit their choice (e.g. to local or school issues). Help students to select one problem. What annoys them the most? Which of the problems do you and they think they could successfully make a change to?

The next step is for students to find out more about their issue. They could use the internet for research, or carry out interviews with other students, family or community members. What sources will be most helpful for their enquiry? What biases can they identify in these sources? What different viewpoints are there on the underlying problem? What has already been done to try and make a change? What do those affected think needs to be done? What do those who oppose change say? What do students think the problem is and what needs to be changed? Why? Students could prepare a briefing sheet or presentation on what they have found out.

Next, students should consider what they could do to make a difference on their chosen issue. This is a chance to get students thinking about all their opportunities for participation; all the actions given in this book. What do students think they can do to make a difference? Encourage students to discuss their ideas, steering them to consider actions they have missed. Alternatively, using this book, groups of students could prepare a short presentation, each on a different type of change action.

Which actions do students think are relevant to their issue? What do they think the impact of their actions will be? Which action do they think would work the best? Which do they think they can achieve? Encourage students to talk to their peers and families, and if possible, those affected, about the impact different actions will have. If they complete more than one action for change, students are mounting their own campaign. How can they combine their campaign actions to achieve their goal most effectively?

Students now need to complete a plan of action. What do they need to do to complete their change action? What is their target date for completion? Can they assign different tasks to different members of the group? What resources do they have available to help them? Can they complete the action in class time, or will they need to organize some element of it out of class or school? Do they need to ask for anyone's help or permission?

When students have completed their action for change, help them to reflect on how effective they were. Ask students to create a display or write a presentation or article on what they have done, to document

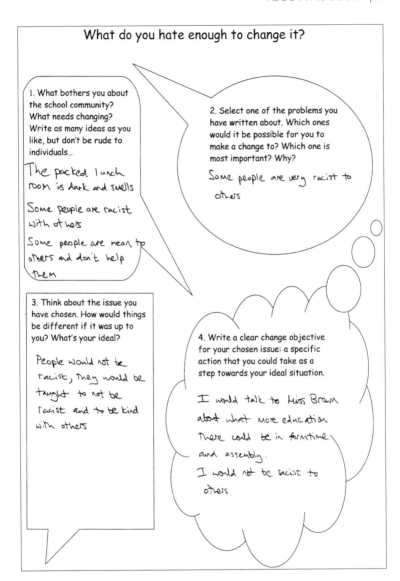

Figure 1.1 *Name*: Barani Ganapathi.
What I think needs changing: Some people make racist comments at school.
The change action I took: Spoke to my form teacher about anti-racist education in form-time, and about taking an assembly.

their work. To what extent did they achieve their aim? Were there any unintended impacts? Did they work well individually or as a team? What would they do differently next time to make their action more effective? Do they think the action they chose has any limitations? What more needs to be done to make the change they want? It will obviously not always be possible for students to change things. If they do not achieve their aim, teachers can encourage students to consider why. They can also help students monitor changes which take place over a long period of time.

The unit of work could be completed by reminding students of the importance of making their voice heard, despite the difficulties and frustrations involved. Using the words of others can help here. Edmund Burke, an eighteenth-century Irish political philosopher, is said to have said, 'All that is necessary for the triumph of evil is that good men do nothing' (he never actually wrote these specific words; they are adapted from his work). Margaret Mead, a twentieth-century cultural anthropologist wrote, 'Never doubt that a small group of thoughtful, committed citizens can change the world. Indeed, it's the only thing that ever has.' Arun Gandhi, the grandson of Mahatma Gandhi, the twentieth-century Indian political and spiritual leader, quoted his grandfather as saying 'We need to be the change we wish to see in the world.'

What might students want to change?

There is no end to the issues young people might want to change, and it is not the job of this book to tell anyone what they should be making a difference to. This book is therefore divided by type of change action (lobbying, donating etc.), to underline the point that students can use the actions in different contexts, and on any issue that is important to them. However, on p. 11 are some ideas to demonstrate the breadth and scope of the issues on which young people may want to campaign. There are strong links between the different contexts of change: many decisions about what happens at school are made at a national level, and most global problems must, in fact, be tackled at local and national levels.

At school

School meals
QUALITY OF TEACHING
Structure of the day
Clubs
Curriculum
Class sizes
Punishments
State of the toilets
Reward system
Uniform
Sports facilities
Break-time arrangements
Trips
Opportunities for student voice

In the local community

Bus services
Parking
Leisure facilities
Libraries
Parks
Schools
Hospitals
Noise pollution
Housing
Planning and building

NATIONALLY

Legal ages, e.g. voting age
The judicial system
Schools' curriculum
Taxes
Foreign policy
Environmental policy
Anti-terrorism measures

GLOBAL

Poverty
Education
Debt of developing countries
Human rights
Spread of disease
Natural disasters
Illegal drugs trade
Global power imbalances
Water scarcity
Fishery depletion
Refugees
Conflicts
Arms trade
Landmines
Trafficking of people
CORRUPT GOVERNMENTS
Terrorism
Power of multinationals
Nuclear armament
Child labour
Child soldiers
Endangered species
Soil degradation
Deforestation
Pollution
Climate change

Take an everyday practical action

Sometimes the power to bring about change lies with someone else. However, it is important that students know that, on some issues, they do directly hold the power to make a difference. Through taking everyday practical actions, making small adjustments to the way they live their lives, they can contribute to change. The difference they make may seem insignificant to them, but across 6.6 billion people on the planet, small changes soon add up; and while the actions may be small, the issues that they tackle are not. Through thinking about the resources they use (see 'Reduce your carbon and ecological footprints', p. 14), and where they spend their money (see 'Use your consumer power', p. 30), young people can impact on huge international problems such as global warming, and the mistreatment of people, animals and the environment. More immediately, by considering their actions towards those around them, they can make a difference in their classroom or family (see 'Take a personal humanitarian action', p. 52).

Many of the actions for change described in this chapter are ideal opportunities for students to make a difference: clearly defined, quick and achievable. Their practical nature means they are different from the actions in other chapters. First, they are relevant to specific problems; they cannot be used flexibly to campaign for change on any issue. Secondly, in most cases students must complete them outside the classroom: around school, at home and out shopping.

However, there are many ways in which students can be supported in class to make a change beyond it. Not everyone agrees on how effective and necessary many of the outlined change actions are. Teachers can encourage students to consider what they think needs changing and why, and the relative merits of different actions. To help teachers do so, this chapter includes explanations of the significance of each action, as well as practical details for carrying them out.

Writing action-pledges or action-diaries can keep up motivation and awareness. Class time could also be used to share student

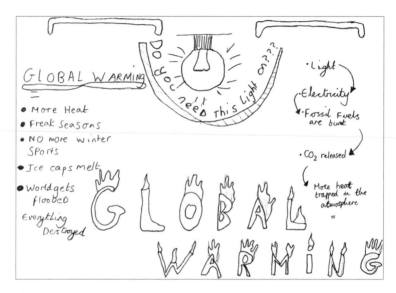

Figure 2.1 *Name*: Owen Donkin.
What I think needs changing: The high level of carbon dioxide in the earth's atmosphere, which is causing global warming.
The change action I took: Made a poster to go by the light switch in the classroom, reminding people to turn off the light when they do not need it on.

achievements. Seeing the actions modelled, or having the opportunity to complete the actions at school, will also help: are the classroom lights and classroom computers off when they are not needed? Is classroom waste recycled?

A different approach is to combine these practical actions with change actions in other chapters, mounting a campaign. For example, in addition to switching off lights themselves, students could raise awareness of the importance of saving energy in this way. Campaign strategies could include designing instructional posters for the school computer room, making announcements in registration time or giving an assembly.

Reduce your carbon and ecological footprints

In their everyday lives students use resources, for example, water, and energy in the form of electricity, gas or petrol. This consumption, and the waste it generates, impacts on the environment, both locally and globally. There are many steps young people can take to reduce their 'footprint' (see 'What are your carbon and ecological footprints and why should you care how big they are?', below). Since most of the resources we consume cost money, many of the change actions in this section could also fit into the section 'Use your consumer power', and vice versa.

What are your carbon and ecological footprints and why should you care how big they are?

Carbon footprint

Your carbon footprint is the amount of carbon dioxide that you are responsible for releasing into the atmosphere.

Forests covered the earth 200 million years ago, and there was a lot of carbon dioxide in the atmosphere. Algae, bacteria, plankton and plants captured carbon dioxide from the air as they converted the energy from the sun into energy for them to grow. As these organisms died, rotted down, and were buried and compacted over thousands of years, they became coal (from plants on land), gas (from algae, plankton and bacteria in the sea) and oil (from fish that ate the sea plants). These 'fossil fuels' are stored, where they were laid down, in the earth's crust.

People discovered that when they burnt these fuels they produced light and heat, releasing the energy that they had trapped from the sun. They found they could be used to warm homes, and power factories and transport. Later, they discovered that they could create electricity from fossil fuels in power stations. The heat released from fossil fuels as they are burnt is used to heat water. The steam created turns turbines which convert movement into electricity. Today we rely on electricity to light our homes and offices, and to power TVs, computers, trains, kettles, and so on. Petrol, used to power our cars and lorries, is derived from oil, as is the fuel used by planes. Between the use of energy as electricity and for transportation, every item we have in our homes (our food, our clothes, our books, our furniture) uses fossil fuels somewhere along its path of production and delivery. Fossil fuels have enabled us to do amazing things.

(Continued)

What are your carbon and ecological footprints and why should you care how big they are?—Cont'd

However, we are discovering that there are two big problems. First of all, fossil fuels are non-renewable or finite. That means that they are going to run out. The second problem is that when we burn fossil fuels they release the carbon dioxide that they stored all those millions of years ago. The increasing level of carbon dioxide (and other gases) in the atmosphere is causing the process of 'global warming'.

Carbon dioxide naturally exists in the atmosphere, and is important because it keeps the planet warm enough for life to exist. It does this by trapping the energy from the sun's rays in the earth's atmosphere, much like a greenhouse does; hence the term 'greenhouse gas'. However, because of the amount of fossil fuels we burn, and the amount of carbon dioxide produced, more and more heat is being trapped in the system. This has, and will, result in the disruption of weather patterns. The well-known warming effect means increased temperatures and, in places, drought. Melting ice-caps will result in rises in sea level and flooding. However, because the climate is complicated, global warming also means more rain and decreased temperatures in some areas, and extreme weather like hurricanes and massive storms. All of these changes threaten people's lives, their livelihoods and their sources of water and food, as well as the environments that animals and plants need to survive.

We have come to rely on fossil fuels, but they are not the only way to produce energy. See 'How should our energy be produced?', p. 21.

Find out more

www.climatechallenge.gov.uk – The government website on climate change.

www.climatecrisis.net – This is the website of Al Gore's film *An Inconvenient Truth*, a documentary on climate change.

www.royalsoc.ac.uk/climateguide – The website of the Royal Society, the national academy of science, draws together information on climate change from leading scientists. This guide tackles common misconceptions and controversies surrounding climate change.

www.stopclimatechaos.org – 'Stop Climate Chaos' is a coalition of lots of different charities and organizations, working together to put pressure on the government to act against climate change.

Ecological footprint

Your ecological footprint is the amount of land and sea that is needed to provide the energy, water, food and other raw materials that you use everyday. It is a broader measure of the resources you use than your carbon footprint. It includes the emissions generated from burning fossil fuels, but also looks at other resources that we use, as well as how much land is required to absorb the waste that we produce.

In July 2007 the world's population reached over 6.6 billion. If everyone in the world used resources in the way that people in many rich countries do, we would need several planets to meet our needs. Your ecological footprint may well be larger than your share: the total of the earth's resources, divided by the 6.6 billion people who need them.

You can calculate your carbon and ecological footprints at:

http://footprint.wwf.org.uk
www.direct.gov.uk/actonco2

Do not use electricity you don't need

Most households and offices waste energy by running appliances when they are not needed. Savings of electricity (and money) can be made by turning things off or down. Can students think of examples? How good are they at turning off the lights when they leave a room? Did they know that the screen saver on computers uses nearly as much energy as when the computer is in use? Or that many chargers,

Fewer of the sun's **MY PLEDGE**
rays get back out
because of Pollution

To reduce the carbon emissions that I am responsible for, I pledge
to reduce the amount of energy I use.

I pledge to: Not to waste hot water, I would have a
shower instead of a bath.

I will take this action: Once a week

Signed: Enobkofo

Figure 2.2 *Name*: Clint Nyongo Ojiendo.
What I think needs changing: Global warming.
The change action I took: Pledged to use less hot water by having a shower instead of a bath at least once a week.

for phones and MP3 players, still use energy when they are plugged into the mains but not charging? Switching off at the mains saves the energy of stand-by lights. What appliances can students think of around their homes that have these little red lights?

Electricity or gas is usually used to heat hot water, so if students use less hot water they are saving energy as well as water. Options include only boiling the amount of water they need in the kettle, and taking a shower instead of a bath.

There are also a number of energy-saving changes which students can encourage their parents to make. These include: mending dripping hot water taps; turning the heating thermostat down instead of opening windows; using the microwave instead of the oven; only running the washing machine or dishwasher when it is full and using the half-load, economy or low temperature settings.

Find out more

www.blackle.com – Blackle™ is a search engine, the screen of which is predominantly black, using less energy than coloured or white screens.

www.est.org.uk – The Energy Saving Trust® offers lots of tips on how to reduce energy waste.

Use electricity more efficiently

Big energy savings can also be made by increasing the efficiency with which electricity, or energy directly from gas or other fossil fuels, is used when it *is* needed.

An easy first step that students can take is to increase the efficiency of their heating system at home by closing their curtains once it gets dark. Heat escapes easily through windows, even if they are closed.

For the other change actions in this section, students will need to persuade their parents to make the change, or at the least get their parents' agreement before they act.

Traditional light-bulbs are not very effective at turning electricity into light; they create a lot of heat as well. Energy-efficient light-bulbs use significantly less electricity and, although they are more expensive than ordinary light-bulbs, over time they can save money. Not only do they use less electricity, but they can also last much longer than ordinary bulbs.

Electrical appliances work more efficiently if they are kept in good working order, for example, by descaling kettles and defrosting freezers regularly.

Let your students know what advice they can give to parents looking to buy a new washing machine, fridge, fridge-freezer or dishwasher. All these white goods have to have an EU energy label which rates their energy efficiency and energy consumption (A+ indicating the most efficient). An easy way to identify the most energy-efficient goods is to look out for the Energy Saving Recommended logo. This scheme, run by the Energy Saving Trust®, endorses A+ rated white goods, as well as energy-efficient lighting appliances, windows, boilers and TVs.

If any of your students are having significant alterations made to their house, or want to take on the challenge of persuading the bill payer to make their home more energy-efficient, there are larger-scale changes they should know about. Can they find out how well covered their home's hot water tanks and pipes are? Good insulation, such as 'jackets' for hot water tanks, can reduce the amount of heat that escapes, allowing the system to heat the radiators or hot water using less electricity (or gas) overall. A well-insulted home also has loft insulation, double glazing and if there are gaps in external walls, cavity wall insulation. Students could also talk to their parents about the type of boiler they have fitted. Condensing boilers are much more efficient at converting energy to heat than conventional ones because they recover a lot of the waste heat which would otherwise be channelled out of the flue and lost.

Interested students can complete a quick questionnaire on the Energy Saving Trust®'s website to see how their home could be more energy-efficient. This site also gives information on grants that are available to make changes.

Find out more

www.est.org.uk – The Energy Saving Trust® website. Lots of ideas on how to increase the energy efficiency of your home.

Find out where your electricity comes from

Most of the electricity in the UK comes from burning fossil fuels. However, there are energy suppliers that harness renewable energy, through wind turbines, solar panels and other technology. 'How should our energy be produced?', p. 21, gives more details on different energy sources.

Every household in the UK is free to choose who supplies their electricity and can switch between suppliers. To raise awareness of this, students could find out which company supplies their electricity at home or school and how it is generated. If they are on a 'green tariff' how much really comes from renewable sources (the company's website will help)? Students committed to making a difference on this issue could research the possible options for their home (including having solar panels fitted as well as changing energy supplier), and lobby their parents to make the change (see Chapter 4 for lobbying actions).

Find out more

www.britishwindenergy.co.uk – The British Wind Energy Association promotes and supports the use of wind energy, and more recently wave and tidal energy.

www.ecotricity.co.uk – An electricity provider that harnesses energy from renewable sources like the wind, the sun and water. They invest in developing new renewable sources like wind farms.

www.good-energy.co.uk – An electricity provider that supplies 100 per cent renewable energy.

How should our energy be produced?

The declining availability of fossil fuels, combined with increases in global energy consumption and the threat of global warming, is leading many individuals and governments to consider the question 'How should our energy be produced?' In other words, what sources of energy should we be using to light and heat our homes and offices, to drive our factories and to run our transport systems? Decisions about where money should be invested to ensure a continued energy supply are controversial. There are a number of alternatives to fossil fuels, all with much debated benefits and problems.

New technology allows us to harness the energy found in the heat of the sun and the earth, and the movement of wind, waves, tides and rivers. The advantage of these 'renewable' energy sources is that they are freely and continually available, and their use involves no release of carbon dioxide.

Geothermal energy is the heat present in some parts of the earth's surface. The centre of the earth is hot because of residual heat from its formation, and the temperature has been maintained by the decay of radioactive substances. In many volcanically active places, where this heat is present near the surface of the earth's crust, water is naturally heated. The resulting steam can be used to drive turbines and generate electricity. Alternatively, wells can be drilled into hot rocks and cold water pumped through them.

Winds are the result of giant currents in the atmosphere, created by the heat of the sun. This 'wind energy' can propel blades on wind turbines, and this motion used to generate electricity.

Energy can be generated from the movement of water in a number of different ways. The energy of waves, produced by the wind dragging on the surface of the sea, can be captured by wave machines. Tidal barrages, where a river

(Continued)

How should our energy be produced?—Cont'd

meets the sea, utilize the kinetic energy of water moving in and out of the river mouth as the tide goes in and out. Hydroelectric power stations work in a similar way, but the energy comes from water released from behind a dam on a river.

Both the heat and light of the sun can be trapped and used. Solar cells convert light into electricity, and solar panels enable hot water to be warmed directly by the heat of the sun.

Although these renewable energy sources provide carbon-dioxide-free sources of energy, and are unlimited, they still have their critics. For example, tidal barrages can damage the habitat of marine species and some people are concerned about noise pollution from wind turbines. Some renewable resources are only available, or suitable on a large scale, in certain places. Others cannot be consistently relied on; for example, wind turbines only work when it is windy, and solar panels only work in the daytime. Finally, at present these sources cannot meet all our energy needs. Sceptics point to the expense of developing the technology, increasing reliability and building the structures needed to provide a greater percentage of the energy we consume.

'Biofuels' are also considered renewable energy resources. This is because they are made from plants, which can, with care, be re-grown. Wood, charcoal and peat have long been used for heating and cooking, but now other fuels can be produced from plant matter. For example, vegetable oil and biodiesel come from the oils and fats in plants, and fermentation can produce alcohols like ethanol and butanol. Crops like wheat, sugar beet and oil palm can be grown specifically to make biofuels. The stalks and leaves of crops grown for other purposes can also be used, along with other waste that normally goes into landfill. Biofuels are burnt to produce energy and are widely used in fuels for cars and other forms of transport.

Theoretically, biofuels are carbon neutral, because the carbon dioxide released when they are burnt is captured when the next crops are grown. However, in reality, this is not the case, because energy is used to fertilize, harvest and transport the crops. However, carbon emissions are likely to be overall lower than those produced by burning fossil fuels. Much more concerning is the pressure that biofuels are putting on land. In some places, crops for biofuel are replacing food crops because they earn the farmer more money, putting food supplies in danger. In other places, rainforest and other habitats are being destroyed to make way for biofuel crops.

Another alternative to fossil fuels is nuclear energy, which is produced through the breakdown of radioactive metals, such as uranium and plutonium, in a process called 'fission'. No carbon dioxide is released, but there are other problems. Leftover nuclear waste remains radioactive and hazardous to health for hundreds or even thousands of years, and accidents at nuclear reactors could be disastrous.

Research is also being carried out into nuclear 'fusion', a potential future energy source. Huge amounts of energy can be produced when two atoms fuse together. Although fusion would still produce potentially harmful waste products, it would do so in much smaller amounts than traditional nuclear energy. It would also be safer than nuclear fission, since it can be more easily stopped. However, at present, a huge amount of money is being poured into this technology, with no certainty about when results will be produced.

Hydrogen is also talked about as an alternative energy source. Hydrogen can make a good fuel because it is light to store, and when burnt produces water as a waste product. However, hydrogen is not found naturally in useful amounts. It has to be made by splitting water into hydrogen and oxygen, and this requires energy from another source. As some of this energy is lost in the splitting process, it is more efficient to use the original source of energy directly. However, hydrogen can be a useful 'transfer medium' when

(Continued)

How should our energy be produced?—Cont'd

the original source, such as a nuclear or solar energy plant, cannot be easily carried around.

Governments around the world are facing important decisions about how their country's energy should be produced. In the UK, the situation is made worse by the fact that many existing fossil fuel and nuclear power stations will be reaching the end of their lifespan in the next ten years. There is concern that this will leave an 'energy gap'. Some see this as an argument for a new generation of nuclear power stations in the UK, while others believe the government should be focusing on reducing energy waste and increasing the use of renewable energy.

Change how you get around

Cars not only give out carbon dioxide in their exhaust fumes, but other polluting gases, such as nitrogen oxide and dark powdery soot. Heavy traffic on the roads also contributes to noise pollution, and injury and death in road accidents.

Encourage students to think about how they could drive, or be driven, less often. Are there times when they could walk or cycle? How does taking public transport, such as the bus or train, or sharing a lift with someone else make a difference?

Find out more

www.sustrans.org – A sustainable transport charity, with lots of information on local cycling routes.

Reuse and recycle

According to the Department for Environment, Food and Rural Affairs (Defra), the UK produces around 330 million tonnes of waste annually, a quarter of which is from households and offices.

Comparing equivalent weights may help students understand the scale of this waste production. The waste produced every hour by households and offices is equivalent to over 1,000 double-decker buses. On average, each person, including young people, generates just over half a tonne of waste per year, the equivalent in weight of a large cow!

Do students know what happens to their rubbish once they throw it out? A small proportion is incinerated, and the majority of it goes into landfill sites. What are the problems with these means of disposal? Incineration can release harmful gases, although it also releases energy, which could be recovered and used, but often is not. In landfill, items which do not degrade will remain there forever and others, which do break down, can release methane, a greenhouse gas, and chemicals that can seep into water supplies. In both cases, the material the item is made from is completely wasted. Some of these materials, like the metals used in mobile phones or the oil used to make plastic, are non-renewable and finite. Not only that, but the electricity and fuel used to make and transport the item are also wasted. All the energy used to collect the raw material, make and shape the product and transport it to where it is needed will have to be used again to replace the item that has been thrown away.

Reusing is one way of reducing waste. It is also the best way because it does not usually involve using much extra energy: the item does not have to be reshaped or transported elsewhere.

What ways of reusing can students think of? Do they or their families already refill empty drinks bottles, use spare plastic bags in their bin instead of buying bin bags or store food in the freezer in old ice-cream tubs? There are products available specifically for reuse. Have they seen their parents using reusable material shopping bags, rechargeable batteries or reusable nappies?

Reusing can also mean using an item, such as a piece of clothing, until it is worn out. This way you do not have to buy a new one for longer, saving all the energy used to make and transport it. Buying one item that will last longer and that you will continue to use is better than buying several versions that quickly break or go out of fashion.

If your students don't think they can reuse an item, then maybe someone else can. Have they ever heard of free-cycling? There is a growing number of websites that allow you to offer unwanted items (like furniture and electrical equipment) for collection and use by someone else in the local community.

If there is no way to keep using an item, the next step is to try and get the material it is made of reused, by recycling it. Do students know if their local council runs a doorstep collection scheme for recycling, and if so, what for? Newspapers and magazines, cards, plastic bottles, glass bottles and jars, aluminium drinks cans, phone directories and junk mail are all commonly collected. Items such as batteries and juice and milk cartons are sometimes more difficult to get recycled. Do students know of collection points they can take these to? What about old printer cartridges (see the change action 'Donate things that you don't need', in Chapter 6)? Some councils also collect food waste, although many households choose to keep this for their own compost heaps.

If student's families already recycle at home, what strategies do they use for sorting rubbish? Where do they store their recycling before it is collected or taken for recycling? What advice could they give on how to use a recycling bin effectively? For example, crushing drinks cans so that more can fit in the bin and separating types of rubbish properly. A good way of modelling this action for change is using recycling points in classrooms and play areas.

Students who don't know what they can get recycled can be pointed to the 'Recycle Now' or 'Recycle-More' websites, which are searchable by postcode for local recycling schemes (see the 'Find out more' section). They can also use these sites to find out who is responsible for their doorstep collection service, and to check which day the recycling should be put out.

Finally, do any of your students buy items made from recycled material? What do they think they can buy that is recycled and what symbol should they find on these products? Students can find out more using the websites that follow.

The good news is that, according to Defra, the amount of household waste recycled or composted in the UK has increased from 6 per cent in 1995–6 to 26 per cent in 2005–6. However, this percentage is still much lower than in many other European countries.

Find out more

www.dontdumpthat.com,www.freecycle.org,www.free2collect.co.uk– Websites which allow the exchange of unwanted goods.

www.recycledproducts.org.uk – The UK directory of recycled products.

www.recycle-more.com – Locate recycling points using this website, and find out about the symbols used on recycled products.

www.recyclenow.com – Searchable for information on local recycling services. Also includes lots of recycling facts and tips.

www.recyclezone.org.uk – Lots of information for students on recycling.

www.recyclingexpert.co.uk – In-depth advice on how to recycle just about anything, and features and articles written by professional journalists and experts.

www.statistics.gov.uk – Facts and figures on waste and recycling in the UK.

Stop junk mail coming to your home

If the recipient is not interested in buying the products or services they offer, mail-outs are wasteful of paper and of the energy used to transport them. Students could try returning unwanted junk mail addressed to them in the pre-paid envelope provided, or by crossing out their name on the envelope and writing 'return to sender'. More effectively, they could contact the Mailing Preference Service, which enables consumers to have their names and home addresses removed from, or added to, lists used by companies that use direct mailing.

Find out more

www.mpsonline.org.uk – The website of the Mailing Preference Service.

Avoid extra packaging

Can students think of examples of products they or their families buy that have heavy or unnecessary packaging? Examples include apples on polystyrene trays wrapped in cling film and ready meals which come in lots of different plastic compartments. Much of this extra packaging is made from plastic, which is difficult to recycle, and so ends up in landfill sites. Challenge students to go food shopping with their parents and see if they can find ways of reducing the amount of packaging they take home with them. Can they buy fruit and vegetables loose rather than pre-packaged? They could also avoid taking supermarket plastic bags by taking their own reusable bags shopping.

Offset your carbon emissions

Offsetting means paying someone to reduce the carbon dioxide in the atmosphere on your behalf, to compensate for the gas emissions your flight, car journey or heating produces. Students can make a donation to a carbon offsetting charity (see Chapter 6, 'Donate'). That money will be used for projects that might include planting trees, enabling households in developing countries to swap their kerosene burners for solar panels or educating people to use energy-efficient light-bulbs.

The benefits of carbon offsetting are contested and it can be worth exploring the issue with students. Some say that carbon offsetting is a real way of helping us think about the contribution we make to carbon emissions, and that the projects funded this way can make a positive difference. Others suggest that offsetting stops us thinking about the damage we are doing. They add that supporting the reduction of carbon dioxide emissions in developing countries is not enough; it is more important that we reduce our own. Critics point to the fact that there is little external regulation in the carbon offsetting industry; it is difficult for buyers to assess the value of 'carbon credits' they buy. Tree planting can be particularly problematic. Large-scale plantations can lead to displacement of people and a reduction in the diversity of wildlife. There is no agreement about how much carbon dioxide trees absorb, and it is hard to ensure that they will not be destroyed or harvested before they reach maturity.

Find out more

www.carbonneutral.com, www.co2.org – Two organizations that allow you to calculate and offset carbon emissions.

www.globalcool.org, www.carbon-offsets.com – Two organizations which will offset for you. Neither use forestry, and both conform to the Gold Standard for carbon credits (www.cdmgoldstandard.org).

Choose your cleaning products carefully

Many detergents and cleaning products are based on petrochemicals, derived from oil. Not only is oil a non-renewable resource, but also the chemicals from such cleaners do not break down well and can build up in the environment where they can cause damage to humans, animals and the environment itself. It is not possible to have a fully environmentally friendly detergent, but there are ecological products available which are less harmful. Can students persuade their families to give them a go? What environmental claims are made by the 'eco' products they already use at home?

Find out more

www.ecover.com – Ecover®, a company which makes ecological detergents and cleansing agents.

Pick up your litter

According to the Environment Agency, the amount of rubbish dropped on our streets has increased by 500 per cent since the early 1960s. Litter, from sweet wrappers to sacks of rubbish, is ugly and causes people to feel less positive about their environment. It can also harm wildlife. Staff from the Royal Society for the Prevention of Cruelty to Animals tackled nearly 12,000 incidents of animals endangered by litter in 2006. Examples include a hedgehog whose head was stuck in a discarded can, a fox whose head was stuck in a car wheel and a duck whose foot was chopped off by fishing line.

What kind of littering do students find particularly offensive? What particular litter problems are there where they live? What litter have they seen on their journey to school? Dog fouling can be a big problem. It is unpleasant and the faeces can contain worm eggs which, if ingested, cause an infection called Toxocariasis, which can result in eye damage. ENCAMS (the organization that runs the Keep Britain Tidy campaigns) is presently particularly targeting littering with cigarette butts, take-away boxes and chewing gum.

Discuss with students the negative impact of littering, challenge them to pick up a piece of litter everyday or support them to organize a litter pick at school or in the local community. Do students know that littering in a public place, including dog fouling, is illegal and carries a fine?

Find out more

www.encams.org – ENCAMS is the environmental charity which campaigns directly to the public, best known for their Keep Britain Tidy campaign.

www.environment-agency.gov.uk – The website of the Environment Agency, the government agency working on environmental issues.

Don't waste water

The UK has a reputation for being rainy, but in fact it has less water available per person than most other European countries. Water is scare in many parts of the country, and to add to the problem, according to the Environment Agency we use almost 50 per cent more water than 25 years ago. Winter is the time when groundwater supplies 'recharge', so if there is a dry winter followed by a hot summer there may be water shortages. Have students experienced a hose pipe ban? The impact of water shortages can be greater for fish, birds and other wildlife.

Being careful with water will mean it is more likely to last through periods of shortage. It also saves on the money and energy used to clean water supplies. Learning to be respectful of water and its value may also be helpful for students visiting parts of the world where water shortage is a more acute problem. Global consumption of water is rapidly increasing, but the amount of fresh water in the world stays the same (though more is being polluted). It is likely that in the future more people will experience water shortages.

How do students think they can save water? What do they already do? Ideas include turning off the tap while brushing their teeth, and using a bowl of water rather than a running tap to wash fruits and vegetables. Encourage students to keep an eye out for drips and leaks. Can they persuade their parents to put a 'hippo' or brick in the toilet cistern so that each flush uses less water, or to invest in a water-butt to collect rainwater for the garden?

Find out more

http://news.bbc.co.uk/1/hi/in_depth/629/629/5086298.stm – This interactive guide from the BBC allows you to calculate the water used in your household and compares it to the UK average.

www.waterwise.org.uk – Waterwise is a UK charity that works to reduce UK water consumption. Information available on the website includes water saving tips and details of the Waterwise Marque, awarded to products which use water efficiently.

Use your consumer power

Young people may have limited financial resources, but that doesn't mean that they can't use the consumer power they have. In particular, they have a lot of persuasive 'pester' power, and can influence the way in which their parents spend. Thinking about what they buy in terms of the impact its production had on the environment is another step that students can take to reduce their carbon and eco-logical footprints. But they can also use their consumer power to make a difference to people, animals and their local communities (see 'What is my consumer power and why should I use it?', below).

What is my consumer power and why should I use it?

By buying from one company or another you are, in effect, financially supporting that company's policies and practices. Thinking about what you buy, in terms of the effect of those policies on the environment, people, and political and eco-nomic systems, is known as ethical consumerism. First, shopping this way gets you what you want – an apple grown without the use of pesticides, or a T-shirt stitched by a decently paid worker. Secondly, it sends out a message about the kind of goods you want to buy. In the end companies are there to make money, and if they think they can make more money by providing their customers with ethically sourced goods, they will. But you have got to show them that this is what you want, by making careful judgements about where you spend your money.

You can choose to spend more money with companies you believe are performing in an ethical way, and not to spend any with companies whose practices you are unhappy about. You can also choose to make your shopping decisions around an issue you are concerned about, such as bad working conditions on plantations (buy fair trade), pollution of water sources (buy organic) or the carbon emissions related to air travel (buy local food). One or more certification schemes exist for many issues like these, so you can make your shop-ping decisions based on the ethical logos that products carry.

Watch out for conflicts between different 'issue' products. It is not always possible to be 'ethical' in every way. For example, some organic products are flown a long way to the UK, racking up 'food miles'. Ethically sourced clothes guar-antee the worker who put them together a fair wage, but not necessarily the worker who grew the cotton.

(Continued)

How should our energy be produced?—Cont'd

Find out more

This chapter includes lots of websites to help you find different 'issue' products. These are some more general ethical shopping websites:

www.ethicalconsumer.org – The website of the Ethical Consumer Research Association, which carries out research into the environmental, animal and human costs of different brands.

www.gooshing.co.uk – An ethical shopping tool from The Good Shopping Guide, which allows you to search a huge range of products and view their 'ethical rating'.

Buy fairtrade products

Many of the foods and drinks we consume everyday, such as tea, coffee, chocolate, and bananas, are grown in developing countries (see 'What is globalization and how does it relate to what I buy?', p. 33, and 'What should I call poor countries?', p. 47). The farmers that grow these crops are often very poor and have no choice but to sell their produce to traders who pay very little. The money they earn can be less than the cost of harvesting the crop, leaving them unable to send their children to school or improve their homes. Farmers who are hired to work on huge farms owned by large international companies, known as plantations, may have further problems like unsafe working conditions, harassment and little job security (see 'What are multinationals?', p. 37). They may not be able to join trade unions (see 'What is a trade union?', p. 91), or take part in decisions that affect their lives on the plantation.

Students may not be aware that one of the major reasons for this situation is the trade laws between countries, which encourage 'free trade' (see 'What is the problem with free trade?', p. 40). In reaction to this, an international movement has been set up called 'fair trade', which promotes standards for how workers and the environment should be treated. Fair trade is trade which ensures that the farmer gets a fair price for what he or she produces (enough to cover the

What is globalization and how does it relate to what I buy?

Globalization is the process of increasing connections between people, companies and countries around the world. These connections are an integral part of what the world is like today. You just need to look at the labels in your clothes or the food packets in your kitchen to get a sense of the range of people and places you are linked to. There are lots of benefits: we can now learn much more about other places, enjoy international foods and products, and work with people in other parts of the world, as well as holiday there.

The major driving force behind globalization is trade, the buying and selling of goods and products. The reason for trade is to obtain different things, but also to make money. This is not necessarily a bad thing: it gives people jobs, and money to spend on food and education, and can drive positive change.

However, two more facts reveal the problem associated with globalization. First, countries and companies will go to huge lengths to keep their profits increasing. Secondly, globalization is occurring in an already imbalanced world. Many countries are extremely poor and their people have little global power. These countries are at a disadvantage when dealing with rich superpowers and their money-making strategies, and are less able to profit from globalization. As the world globalizes a minority of people are getting very rich from international trade, and people in developed countries are gaining access to cheap products from around the world. At the same time, exploitation by multinationals and unfair international trade laws mean that many people in poor countries are, in fact, getting poorer (see 'What are multinationals', p. 37, and 'What is the problem with free trade?', p. 40).

costs of production and guarantee an income they can live on), and better working conditions.

Do students know what the Fairtrade mark looks like? It is awarded by the Fairtrade Foundation. What fairly traded products do they think they can buy or have they bought before? Their answers might include chocolate, coffee, tea, nuts, fruit and fruit juice, honey, rice, flowers, wine, beer, spices, footballs, and clothes made from fairly traded cotton. Do students know where they can buy these products? Are any of them stocked at school?

Your students might want to know why fair trade is sometimes seen as controversial. Many people believe that buying fairtrade products is a positive way of using consumer power to express a wish for greater justice in the production of goods. Others think that it is a way of making us feel better that doesn't sufficiently challenge the current trading system, based on 'free trade'.

Find out more

www.bafts.org.uk – The website of the British Association for Fair Trade Shops.

www.bananalink.org.uk – Banana Link campaigns for a fair and sustainable banana trade.

www.blackgoldmovie.com – The website of *Black Gold*, a film highlighting ethical issues surrounding the coffee industry.

www.fairtrade.org.uk – The website of the Fairtrade Foundation that awards the Fairtrade mark to fairly traded products. Find out here what fairtrade products you can buy and where you can buy them.

www.traidcraft.co.uk – Traidcraft runs a business selling fairtrade products and a charity which works to improve the lives of producers.

Buy organic products

The word organic is controlled by law; any food labelled organic must meet strict standards. Organic farmers severely restrict their use of chemical fertilizers and pesticides, instead developing a healthy soil by growing a mixture of crops. The production of agrochemicals and fertilizers uses a lot of energy, so organic farming means lower carbon dioxide emissions. Using fewer chemicals reduces the chance of them seeping into the groundwater (from which they are expensive to remove), and leads to a greater diversity of birds, butterflies and plants on organic farms. Organic farmers must not routinely use drugs on their animals, which are kept in more natural conditions. Some people think organic food tastes better too.

Have students seen any organic symbols on foods? Organizations like the Soil Association and the Organic Food Federation guarantee that foods that carry their logo are produced to organic standards. Do they know that as well as organic fruit, vegetables and meat, it is also possible to buy organic biscuits, wine and cheeses? There is also a big range of non-food organic products, such as clothing, towels, bedding, mattresses and skin care, made from materials that have been grown organically.

Find out more

www.orgfoodfed.com – The Organic Food Federation certifies organic food products.

www.soilassociation.org – The Soil Association promotes organic farming and its symbol is a well recognized trademark for organic produce.

www.theorganicdirectory.co.uk – A guide to everything organic, produced by the Soil Association.

Buy products from sustainable sources

Unlike fossil fuels, animals and plants are renewable resources; their populations can replace or sustain themselves, allowing us to continue to use them for food, building materials, clothes and medicines. However, they are fragile resources, because if humans treat them badly, their sustainability can be seriously damaged.

As well as avoiding items which are more likely to come from unsustainable sources, it is possible to buy wood products and fish from sources that are certified as being managed to ensure they can re-grow or reproduce. Except perhaps for some paper products, students are unlikely to buy these items regularly themselves. They may, however, be able to influence their parents' spending.

Emphasize that it is particularly important to take care when buying hardwood products. Tropical hardwoods come from tropical rainforest, ancient ecosystems rich in plants and animals, which are being rapidly destroyed by logging. Concerned students should look out for the logo of the Forest Stewardship Council (FSC), a tree with a tick on it. FSC-certified products, which have been made from trees cut in a legal and sustainable manner, include garden furniture, decking, sheds, conservatories, tools, bird boxes and bird tables, brushes, wallpaper, flooring, doors, shelves, furniture, toilet tissue, paper (including some books) and pencils. The PEFC™ Council (Programme for the Endorsement of Forest Certification schemes) is a global umbrella organization for forest certification schemes worldwide.

Logging is not the only pressure on rainforest. Land is cleared to make room for farming, including crops and grazing for cattle. It is much harder to identify products grown on rainforest-cleared land, which can include widely used foods such as beef and palm oil. Can students find out what the causes of rainforest destruction are in different countries? Can they identify anything they eat which may have come from rainforest-cleared land? Can they be sure?

There is also a Stewardship Council for fish (the Marine Steward-ship Council or MSC), which was set up to find a solution to the problem of falling fish stocks. Many fish species are being over-fished. Problems include methods that take small fish along with bigger ones, so that these younger fish don't live long enough to spawn. The MSC has developed an environmental standard for sustainable and well-managed fisheries, which is the main fisheries-certification scheme which exists. Fish products produced to their standards carry their logo.

Students may already be aware of the threat that fishing can pose to dolphins. 'By-catching' is a term for non-target species that are caught, and dolphins are a common 'by-catch'. 'Dolphin-friendly' tuna is caught using a long multi-baited line dragged behind a ship, instead of a net. How many of your students know whether the tuna they normally eat at home is labelled 'dolphin-friendly'? Students concerned about the welfare of marine species may want to know that such labelling is, in fact, controversial. There is no universal independent inspection programme to verify and accredit dolphin-friendliness. In addition, there is evidence that 'long-lining' is devastating to turtles, sharks, albatross and other seabird species, and that fishing boats can still separate dolphin calves from their mothers.

Find out more

www.fsc-uk.org – The website of the Forest Stewardship Council. Find out about their work, and search their database for wood products which comply with their standards.

www.msc.org – The website of the Marine Stewardship Council, and go to http://eng.msc.org/ to find out which MSC-certified fish products are available in the UK.

What are multinationals?

Multinationals are companies which trade in many countries. Their logos, on the food, drinks and clothes they sell around the world, are a symbol of globalization. Many multinationals make more money each year than some of the world's poorest countries. They make big profits by keeping their costs low. This means that some of them are prepared to exploit their workers and mistreat the environment. They are also so huge and powerful that they are able to persuade governments to make decisions in their favour. Through the huge amount they can spend on advertising they can get hold of the public's attention and manipulate the way they think about what they buy. That can make it difficult for us not to buy their products, because those around us see them as marks of fashion or status.

www.panda.org – The website for the World Wide Fund for Nature, or WWF. Find out more about marine and forest habitat destruction.

www.pefc.org – The PEFC™ (Programme for the Endorsement of Forest Certification schemes) is a global umbrella organization for forest certification schemes.

Buy locally grown produce

Ask students to look in their food cupboards at home, or go food shopping with their parents, and create a list of foods they eat and where they come from. They could use an atlas to map the journey of their food. Can they add up the total distance travelled by the items in their family's weekly shop or the foods that make up a chosen meal? Which food on their list travelled the furthest to get to them?

The term 'food miles' has been coined to refer to this distance, from producer to consumer. Why do they think the distance matters? One element of globalization is that many foods available in the UK are produced elsewhere and then transported to their destination (see 'What is globalization and how does it relate to what I buy?', p. 33). This requires fuel to be burnt by lorries, ships or planes, and the release of greenhouse gases (see 'What are your carbon and ecological footprints and why should you care how big they are?, p. 15). Examples include butter from New Zealand and oranges from Spain.

Can students think of any factors, other than the distance, that might determine the environmental impact of the food's journey? What about the type of transport or the quantity in which the food has been transported? Do they think it is possible to tell if an item has been flown, shipped or driven?

Air travel is often pointed to as particularly environmentally damaging. Airlines would argue that their contribution to global carbon dioxide emissions is relatively small, but aviation is one of the fastest growing contributors. In addition, the fact that aircraft release their emissions high in the atmosphere is thought to increase the global-warming impact of some of the gases they emit. This is thought to be true for gases such as nitrogen dioxide, but not for carbon dioxide. The total global-warming impact of aviation is therefore difficult to calculate, but is certainly rising.

Locally produced foods generally accumulate far fewer 'food miles'. They are also likely to be fresh, and money spent on them goes to local farmers and producers (see change action 'Buy from local traders', in this chapter). Can students think of changes they would have to make to their diet if they only ate local produce? Can they think of examples of foods that are grown in Britain, but only at some times of year? Shopping locally means learning to cook and eat what is in season and not expecting to be able to eat everything all year round.

There are also lots of foods that it is not possible to grow locally at all, like cocoa and tea. Emphasize to students that watching the miles their food accumulates is not about never buying anything from abroad; it is about considering ways of reducing the environmental impact of what they eat. For example, could they persuade their parents to buy lamb reared in the UK rather than in New Zealand, and local apples rather than ones flown in from Chile? What advice would they give their parents if buying local lamb meant driving half an hour to go and pick it up?

Find out more

www.farmersmarkets.net – A directory of farmers markets, inspected to ensure that they are genuinely markets where farmers, growers or producers from the local area are present to sell their own produce, direct to the public.

Take a stand on genetically modified foods

Genetically modified (GM) foods are produced from genetically modified organisms (GMOs). The GMOs have had their genetic material altered in a way that does not occur naturally. Genetic material, or DNA, is taken by scientists from one organism and put into the genetic make-up of another organism. This can give the recipient organism new and useful traits. For example, tomatoes can be modified to make them more resistant to rotting, and maize can be modified to give it extra proteins, making it better for animal feed.

There is a huge amount of controversy surrounding genetic modification, and students need to be aware of GM products they are buying, and consider whether they are happy to do so now, or in the future. Teachers can support students to take a stand either way, by helping them understand the pros and cons.

Supporters of the use of GMOs say that they could benefit the environment. Pesticides are energy-heavy to make, and can build up harmfully in soil and waterways. Crops modified to be pest-resistant require fewer such chemicals. Others point to the potential GM foods have to tackle poverty and starvation with crops engineered to grow in difficult conditions.

Critics argue that the benefits of GM are unlikely to go to the poor, but to rich biotech companies. They state that we do not yet understand enough about how genes work to start using GMOs. The long-term impacts on the environment and human health are unknown. There is concern that GMOs could spread through nature and interbreed with natural organisms in a way that cannot be controlled.

There are currently no GM crops being grown in the UK. However, they have previously been grown for research and development purposes, and the government has not banned their commercial use in the future. Some countries do allow the use of this technology at the moment, and so some products sold in the UK contain GMOs. Students concerned about genetic modification should look carefully at their food labels. All foods that contain ingredients produced from GMOs must have this indicated on the label, and GM products sold 'loose' should have this information displayed next to the food.

Find out more

www.defra.gov.uk – The website of the government Department for Environment, Food and Rural Affairs. Find out more about the government's position on the use of GMOs.

www.greenpeace.org – Greenpeace is against the use of GMOs, and
you can read its arguments here.

What is the problem with free trade?

Free trade is when countries trade with each other without
any barriers. That means that any company can sell as much
of what they want, in any country they want. The theory is
that if all barriers are removed then trade will drive economic
growth, which in turn will create wealth. This should mean
that countries are able to produce what they are best able to
grow or make, and sell it, getting money to buy what is better
produced elsewhere.

Unfortunately, in reality it doesn't work like this. Poor countries often have new industries which are struggling to grow
and develop. Free trade laws mean that the government is not
allowed to help these infant industries by making payments
to them (subsidies). In contrast, companies in rich countries
are well developed and have the advantages of new and
expensive technology. They can make products more cheaply
than the industries in poor countries.

The governments of poor countries cannot stop these cheap
goods being sold in their countries. Free trade laws do not
allow them to set limits on the amount of a good that can be
imported (quotas), or taxes which companies have to pay to
import a good (tariffs). Local people, often poor themselves,
buy the imports because they are cheap instead of giving
their business to local industries, which then struggle to grow
and expand.

So why, if it makes it more difficult for them, do poor countries go along with 'free trade'? Lots of poor countries owe
money to rich countries and international organizations, or
need their help in other ways, so pressure can be put on them
to drop their subsidies, quotas and tariffs. Also, being less rich
and powerful, they have less say in how international trade
laws are determined.

To make the situation worse for poor countries, rich countries themselves do not always listen to the 'rules' of free
trade. They continue to subsidize their farmers and industries

and to protect their own markets. So in reality 'free trade' doesn't exist anyway.

Many people believe that trade laws should, at least, be fair; they should not be giving an advantage to companies and countries that are already rich and getting richer. Some think that they should be more than even: that they should give an advantage to poor countries that start at a disadvantage.

Find out more

www.maketradefair.com – The website of the Oxfam campaign to make trade laws fair.

Make sure your clothes are ethically sourced

Ethical trade can mean all types of business that promote more socially or environmentally responsible trade. This broad definition would include fair trade, organic and non-animal tested products. The terms ethical trade or ethical sourcing are sometimes used more specifically to refer to trade that ensures that labour standards are respected all the way along the supply chain. That means that the workers who made the product are treated well and paid a decent wage.

As the world has become more globalized, more of the clothes we buy in the UK are made in developing countries such as Bangladesh, Indonesia, China and Vietnam (see 'What is globalization and how does it relate to what I buy?',p. 33, 'What are multinationals?', p. 37, and 'What should I call poor countries?', p. 47). What countries of origin can students find on the labels of their clothes? Retail companies in the UK do not generally own the factories in developing countries where their clothes are made. They contract out the work directly, or indirectly through buyers, to the factory owners. The main reason for this 'outsourcing' is that it is possible to pay workers lower wages in developing countries than in the UK. In addition, the laws about how workers must be treated may be less strict.

These factories provide jobs to local people, who might otherwise be unemployed. However, conditions may be bad, with long hours, forced overtime, lack of job security and harassment. Workers can suffer from poor health, exhaustion and stress. Pay is often below what is needed for a decent standard of living, and trade unions may be prohibited (see 'What is a trade union?', p. 91). Factories like this are sometime called sweat-shops.

Students can find out more about sweat-shop conditions and which shops use these factories by looking at the campaigning websites below. Students could carry out research with the aim of writing an imagined diary entry for a sweat-shop worker or putting together a case study on the sweat-shop use of a chosen retailer.

To be completely sure that what they buy has been made by people who have been treated decently, they will need to look out for companies that specifically sell ethically sourced clothing. Do they know of any? Can they find any on the internet? What claims do these companies make about how they source their clothing? Would students be interested in buying any of their clothes? Encourage students to consider what factors affect their choice of clothes other than the conditions of the people who made them (e.g. fashion, 'coolness'). Why do people often value these factors more? What needs to change to make the situation different?

Find out more

www.cleanclothes.org, www.labourbehindthelabel.org, www. nosweat.org.uk – The Clean Clothes Campaign, Labour behind the Label and No Sweat: three campaigning organizations which work to improve working conditions in the global garment industry.

Avoid products tested on animals

Animal testing affects millions of animals every year. Organisms from fruit flies to monkeys are used in experiments to find out more about how they behave, develop and function, and to safety test drugs, vaccines and cosmetics.

Animal testing is an emotive issue for many students, and an extremely controversial one. Supporters say that animal research plays a vital role in medical advance, and that alternative methods of testing are not sufficiently developed. According to UK law, all new drugs must be tested on animals before they can be used by humans. There are laws in place to protect the animals used for this purpose. However, opponents claim that there are alternatives to animal testing, that testing human products on animals is poor scientific practice or that animals have a right not to be treated in this way.

Many people find animal-testing cosmetics, like lipsticks and skin creams, particularly offensive. It is not legal to carry out this kind of testing in the UK, though at present it is still legal in the EU (though this will be phased out from 2009). However, many cosmetics companies buy their products from abroad where animal testing for cosmetics is legal, and many major brand names are not UK-based.

Students who want to avoid products tested on animals should look out for the leaping bunny symbol. This indicates that the product conforms to the Humane Cosmetics Standard or the Humane Household Product Standard. Companies approved by these standards do not conduct or commission animal testing for their cosmetics, toiletries or household products. These standards were launched by a coalition of animal protection groups, including BUAV, the British Union for the Abolition of Vivisection (vivisection is the dissection of a living organism).

Students who are against animal testing should be aware of a minority of fellow activists whose actions amount to terrorism. The UK laws governing animal experiments are among the strictest in the world. However, for some campaigners this is not enough, and they are prepared to break the law, damage property and hurt people to make their point. Scientists have been threatened and intimidated. Shareholders in organizations that use animal testing, and the relatives of staff-members, have been targeted. For many, this use of violence against people is an unacceptable method of lobbying.

Find out more

www.buav.org – The website of the British Union for the Abolition of Vivisection.

www.co-operative.co.uk – The Co-op brand non-food products are not tested on animals by the Co-op or their suppliers. The Co-op campaigns against animal testing and maintains a website on animal testing issues.

www.gocrueltyfree.org – Find products that have been approved under the Humane Cosmetics Standard and the Humane Household Products Standard.

www.peta.org.uk – PETA (People for the Ethical Treatment of Animals) is a hard-line animal rights organization that opposes all forms of animal use for food, clothing, entertainment, experimentation or any other reason.

Buy from local traders

There are two main reasons to buy from local traders, such as green-grocers, butchers, or in fact any shop that is not part of a big chain. First, you can be sure that the money is going to go back into the local community. Big national or multinational chains may hire local staff, but the profits from the company may not stay locally (see 'What are multinationals?', p. 37). In this way, many of the UK's largest companies derive a large fraction of their income from stores abroad, as well as throughout the UK.

Secondly, spending money with local traders supports a variety of shops and prevents a monopoly, a situation where there is only one provider of a product in an area. Big companies are often able to provide products cheaply because they are operating on a large scale. They can dictate terms to farmers and shippers because they buy so much at once. Their size also allows them to be more convenient, providing a range of different products in the same place, as well as good parking, cafes and other facilities. However, if everyone does their shopping at these big stores, local businesses, that find it difficult to compete because they do not have the advantages of size, will be forced out of business. This is already happening in many places.

As companies get bigger, they get more powerful. In their quest to increase their profits, they may not always act in ways that benefit suppliers, workers, the local community or the environment. They may have the money and power to pressure individuals, local authorities and governments to let them do this. For example, many large companies in the UK make substantial donations to political parties. Why do students think it might be dangerous for a big company like this to have a monopoly? If there is nowhere else to shop it is difficult for consumers to use their consumer power to protest against the actions of the company.

How many local shops, which are not part of a chain, can your students list? What products do they stock? Is there anything they can buy there that, at the moment, they are buying from big chains? The convenience and price of supermarkets is a lure for everyone. The relative merit of shopping in local stores versus supermarkets makes a good debate. Try the motion 'This house believes that shopping in a supermarket is the best way to do the weekly shop.'

Holiday ethically

Your students are unlikely to be able to decide exactly where they want to go on holiday and which company they go with. However, they may well have a say in family holiday plans, and all students can think about how to be a more responsible tourist wherever they go.

The topic could be introduced by discussing the growth of the tourism industry. What factors mean people are taking more holidays and going further? What are the benefits of tourism for an area? Tourists, or visitors to a place, need places to stay and eat, transport to get them around and things to do. They can bring a lot of money into an area. What about the problems? If tourism isn't well managed it can lead to overcrowding, and damage to the environment. Pollution and rapid construction of badly planned buildings can have a negative impact on the very thing the tourists came for in the first place, whether that is a beach, a rainforest or a historical city centre.

In developing countries the problems can be even more acute. Tourists can cause offence to locals by breaking codes of dress and conduct. Relaxed local laws on construction and waste disposal can mean that environmental and aesthetic damage is acute. Can students think of any examples from their own holiday experiences?

In addition, a lot of the money made from package holidays and foreign-owned resorts does not stay in developing countries, but ends up in the pockets of businesses in wealthy countries. Often furnishings, foods and drinks are imported, and the manager and better paid staff are not local. Local people may have jobs, but they can be poorly paid. Hotels, with their swimming pools and air conditioning, use resources such as water and electricity which may be in short supply locally.

In reaction to this, there is a growing 'eco-tourism' movement. Some travel agents, tour operators and hotels have policies on the way they treat the local people and environment. These policies may include use of local staff and produce, strategies for reducing environmental impact, and contributions to local conservation and community projects. Some people say that these policies also ensure that you get a better holiday. By working closely with local people and the environment, eco-holidays are more likely to provide an insight into the eco-system and culture visited.

There is no one global accreditation scheme for eco-tourism, but there are a number of different schemes that recognize companies that act responsibly. Students can research these schemes and their eco-holiday options using the websites below as a starting point. An additional 'ethical' consideration to take into account is the carbon dioxide producing 'air miles' involved.

Once on holiday, what do students think they can do to be responsible tourists? Disposing of litter carefully, and conserving water and electricity are just as important on holiday as at home, if not more so. Can they make sure they buy locally made food, drink and gifts so that they know that the money is going to local people? They should be aware that buying souvenirs made from tortoise-shell, ivory and coral contributes to the destruction of endangered species. To get the most out of their holiday, and reduce the chances of causing offence, what can they find out about local culture before they go?

Find out more

www.aito.co.uk – The Association of Independent Tour Operators has guidelines on responsible tourism for its members, and has a star classification system for progress made.

www.greenglobe21.com – A worldwide benchmarking and certification programme for the travel and tourism industry.

www.tourismconcern.org.uk – A charity that fights exploitation in the tourist industry. They work with communities in destination countries to reduce social and environmental problems connected to tourism and with the outbound tourism industry in the UK to find ways of improving tourism so that local benefits are increased.

www.tourismfortomorrow.com – Tourism for tomorrow awards, awarded by the The World Travel & Tourism Council.

Invest your money carefully

This is a difficult change action for most school students. The chances are that either they will not have a bank account or which bank their account is with will have been decided for them. However, understanding the difference they can make with their investment choices will be really important as they start earning, and there may be some students who want to, and are able to, make a change sooner.

To do so, they will need to understand a little about how banks work. What do students think happens to money they deposit in

What should I call poor countries?

As well as being called poor, less wealthy countries are sometimes termed developing, less economically developed, Third World and countries of the South. Rich countries are also called developed, more economically developed, First World and countries of the North.

There is a lot of discussion about which terms are best, and there is no one right answer. In this book the terms rich and poor, and developed and developing are used because, in the context, they are the clearest. Before you choose a term, think about what the term means and which you are most comfortable using.

The disagreement over which term should be used results from controversy over what development itself is. At its most basic, the term development means growth and change. You can talk about a baby developing into an adult, or an acorn developing into a tree. However, although we know that babies develop into adults, and acorns into trees, people disagree about what countries are developing towards or into.

For some people, development is becoming more like today's richer countries. Others think that we should not see development as a ladder with rich countries at the top. They are unhappy with the terms developed and developing, because they indicate that some countries are further towards a goal that has been specified by rich countries. They add that no country can be called developed; there is always necessary change and growth occurring. The terms First World and Third World also indicate that richer countries come ahead of poorer countries. These are also outdated terms because they refer to a time when many countries were communist and referred to as Second World.

Some see development as about becoming richer. Others think that it is about much more than money; about improving people's quality of life. So instead of measuring wealth, you should measure factors like the number of children who get educated, the number of doctors, the number of people

(Continued)

What should I call poor countries?—Cont'd

with access to safe water or the number of people who can read and write. Obviously, having more money helps improve these factors, but some poor countries have been able to make big improvements to people's quality of life, while in some rich countries some people (particularly women) do not have all the things they need. So, perhaps the terms rich and poor are too simplistic. They do not tell us about the quality of people's lives, and they refer only to money, not to wealth of culture and heritage. In the same way, some see the terms more economically developed and less economically developed as too money-focused.

One way of avoiding all these issues is to use the terms 'countries of the North' and 'countries of the South'. However, these terms are not terribly accurate. After all, Australia is geographically in the South, and is a rich or developed country. Critics of these terms also point to the fact that while the issue of what development means is extremely challenging, it is also very important and should not be side-stepped altogether.

the bank? Banks lend it to other people and companies, who must pay it back with interest. They also buy and sell companies or parts of companies. Banks invest in a huge range or corporations around the world. This may include companies students are unhappy about, for example, arms manufacturers and companies with poor human rights records.

Some banks have ethical policies about where they lend their money. Wherever students choose to invest they should make sure they read the small print about how their money will be used.

Find out more

www.co-operativebank.co.uk – Currently the only bank with branches on high streets that has a published ethical policy. Their policy states that no funds will be lent to any government or business that fails to uphold basic human rights, or whose links to oppressive regimes are a continuing cause for concern.

www.ecology.co.uk – The Ecology Building Society offers mortgages, but only for building and renovation work that respects the environment. You can also get a savings account here.

www.ethicalinvestors.com – The Ethical Investors group provides advice on where to invest your money ethically.

www.triodos.co.uk – Triodos Bank finances companies, institutions and projects that add cultural value and benefit people and the environment.

Complain if there is a problem with something you buy

Students who are aware of their consumer rights can take action if there is a problem. In doing so they can avoid being exploited, protect other consumers and improve the standards of trade.

What do students think their rights are when they buy something? In what circumstances do they think they have a right to a refund or exchange? See 'What are my consumer rights?', p. 50, for a summary of consumer rights. What would they do if they were refused a refund, exchange or compensation they think they are entitled to? Emphasize the importance of dealing with the shop in the right way. When making a complaint about a product, students should go equipped with a clear understanding of the facts (including when the item was bought, and what they think the outcome of their complaint should be). If they are still unhappy with the response they get they could ask to speak to the manager, keeping calm and polite. It is in the shop's interests to keep their customers happy, so hopefully the problem will be resolved at this stage. However, in case not, it is worth keeping a record of what was said and by whom.

Do your students know what to do next if they feel their rights have not been met? First, they could formalize their grievance by writing to the shop manager (or if it is a chain, the company head office). See p. 80 for letter writing tips. Alternatively, they could make a complaint online via howtocomplain.com, which channels emails directly to companies in their database (see the 'Find out more' section).

If they are still not happy with the response they receive, students should seek advice on what to do next. Their local Citizens Advice

What are my consumer rights?

When you buy something you are entering into a contract. This contract gives you some basic, or statutory, rights. Wherever you buy from (whether a shop, street market or mail-order catalogue), you can expect the following:

◆ that the product matches the description given; this means it must be the same as the description on the packaging, on the advert or given by the assistant in the shop;
◆ that the product is of satisfactory quality; this means it must be free from faults and not scratched or damaged, unless this was pointed out at the time of sale;
◆ that the product is fit for its purpose; this means it must be able to do what it is intended for.

If you are paying for a service, such as a hairdresser, you can expect the competent performance of the operator, and that the service is carried out with reasonable care and skill, in reasonable time and for a reasonable price.

If the seller fails to meet these implied conditions, they are in breach of contract. Traders cannot get around this by saying 'the manufacturer is responsible', 'the management does not accept responsibility' or 'we do not offer refunds'.

If something you buy is faulty, and you take it back promptly you should get your money back. The exact amount of time you have is not specified by law but is commonly quoted as a month. You can accept a repair or replacement at this stage, but you can still get your money back later if this also goes wrong.

If you take the item back for the first time after a month, or the fault develops later, you may have to agree to a repair, replacement or partial refund. You never have to accept a credit note if you do not want to.

If you are provided with a poor service, you are not normally entitled to a refund, but either a reduction in the cost for the job or free repairs. If, as a result of faulty goods or services, you are injured or your property is damaged, you are entitled to compensation.

You do not need a receipt to claim your rights, but you do have to be able to prove where you bought the good or service, and a receipt is the easiest way to do so.

Increasingly, shops offer additional services such as changing products that are not faulty (e.g. exchanging a jumper for a different size or colour). This is up to the shop; it is not your right.

Find out more

www.askcedric.org.uk – A consumer education resource and information centre, from Cambridgeshire County Council.
www.consumerdirect.gov.uk – Provides detailed information on consumer rights.

Bureau or the advisors at Consumer Direct can help. If necessary, they will be able to support students to make a complaint to the Trading Standards Department, who are responsible for enforcing consumer law.

Find out more

www.citizensadvice.org.uk – The Citizens Advice Bureau offers advice on many issues, including consumer problems. Many of their offices have legal specialists.
www.consumerdirect.gov.uk – Provides detailed information on consumer rights and advice on how to complain. You can also contact their advisors by phone or email to get advice.
www.financial-ombudsman.org.uk – The website of the body responsible for addressing complaints about financial services like banks.
www.howtocomplain.com – Allows you to make an email complaint to a large number of organizations, as well as providing advice on how to complain to companies not in their database. There is also information on regulators and advice centres you can contact.
www.tradingstandards.gov.uk – The Trading Standards Department website. Search for local Trading Standards offices by postcode.

Take a personal humanitarian action

An action can be called humanitarian if it has the interests of mankind at heart. That means helping other people, and not necessarily because of personal ties, but because of a belief in the right of every human to respect and dignity.

What images come to mind for your students when they hear the term 'humanitarian action'? Can they think of any examples? Often when people use the term, they are referring to projects and strategies to help people suffering as a result of crises like droughts, floods or earthquakes. It is often used to refer to aid given to developing countries (see 'What should I call poor countries?', p. 47).

However, humanitarian action is not limited to helping people far away, or helping the very poorest. The backdrop is much less dramatic, and it may not always be easy or comfortable, but humanitarian action starts at home. There are many ways that your students can act to help those around them; this section includes some ideas.

Talk to someone who might need some help

Young people are generally very good at coming up with small everyday ways they can make other people's lives better. They might suggest asking someone how they are, complimenting or making a positive comment, offering a listening ear and advice, or giving some practical help. While they are often very compassionate in offering this support to their friends, they are not always as good at seeing the needs of those outside their group. You could challenge your students to offer a small humanitarian gesture towards someone they would not normally think of helping.

Many schools have schemes which help some students develop skills to support their peers, including befriending or buddying. In some schools older students are given the job of looking out for students in younger year groups and ensuring that the transition from primary school is smooth. Other schools train 'peer educators', who help other students learn more about a particular subject, or support those who need extra help. Why might some students need and benefit from this type of support?

If students think their friend or peer needs more support than their friends and family can offer alone, there are people who can help. If they would prefer to speak to someone outside the situation, and in confidence, they could try the Samaritans or Child Line phone lines.

You could broaden the discussion here to consider where help comes from in society. Ask students if they can think of times in their life when they do need help outside of their friends and family. What if they are unwell? Where would they go to for help? Do they know how doctors' surgeries and hospitals are paid for? Can they think of other services that local and national government provide them (see 'How is the country run?', p. 72). Do students think that it is a good thing that the government provides these kinds of services? How do they pay for them? Do they know of any organizations or places they could go to for help that are not run by the government? What about faith groups? What about charities, like the NSPCC that runs Childline? Can students think of other examples of voluntary sector organizations? What kind of help do they offer? Where do they get their money from? For more information on charities, see Chapter 6.

Find out more

www.charitycommission.org.uk – The Charity Commission's website lists all registered charities and the areas that they work in.

www.childline.org.uk – Childline is a free helpline for children and young people.

www.gogivers.org – Go-Givers is a primary school website from the Citizenship Foundation aimed at developing an understanding of and commitment to giving in all its forms.

www.kidscape.org.uk – Kidscape works to provide children, parents and organizations with the skills and resources to prevent bullying.

www.redbox.gov.uk – An interactive site encouraging students to consider how the government makes tax and public spending decisions.

www.samaritans.org.uk – The Samaritans offers a free 24 hour confidential phone line for people experiencing feelings of distress or despair.

Resolve a conflict

Conflicts, oppositions of ideas or interests, are natural and can be the stimulus for creativity. They are ways of working through problems to make changes and allow growth.

Students can learn how to communicate better at times of conflict. Explaining clearly what the problem is and listening to the other side of the argument allows those involved to work towards a solution, rather than slipping into damaging aggression and violence. Strategies students can adopt include: waiting until they have calmed down before they confront the other person; avoiding aggressive and confrontational body language (like crossed arms); and explaining how they feel and what they need now rather than blaming the other person. They will also need to learn to value their relationships more highly than 'being right' and to forgive.

Students may be able to 'mediate' conflicts between their friends and family members by helping those involved communicate better. Can they see underlying patterns in the way those involved behave towards each other that keep leading to conflict? What changes could they make to stop this? If one person has done something particularly hurtful, how could they 'put it right'? Some schools train peer mediators to help other students work through their disagreements.

Talking about personal conflict provides an opportunity to reflect on conflict on a larger scale: national and international wars and terrorism. What are the reasons behind such armed and violent conflict? Are students aware that at their core there are often similar issues to the ones they fight over with friends and family? Like individuals, countries and groups of people fight about what belongs to them, particularly land. They conflict because they do not like what they are being told to do, think that they are being treated unfairly or because they have different beliefs.

Find out more

www.crispuk.org – CRISP is an organization that runs peer mediation training in schools.

www.ppu.org.uk – The Peace Pledge Union is a pacifist organization that campaigns against war and educates for peace.

Get to know someone else or another way of being

Hatred is born out of misunderstanding. What do your students think this means? People feel frightened and threatened by things that are different and that they do not understand, and this can lead to dislike and conflict. Can students give examples of stigmas and stereotypes that lead to discrimination? What differences are these perceptions based on? Do students know what a 'scapegoat' is? Why do people take out their fear or pain on people who are 'different' in some way?

If students learn more about someone else's beliefs and ways of being they can tackle their own negative perceptions of other people. They are more likely to understand another's actions and not take offence, and less likely to find what they do strange and intimidating. They may even find that what they learn makes sense, is interesting, casts light on something they had not thought about before, and helps them reconsider their own identity and values. They might also find out how painful being discriminated against can be.

Students can get to know about other religions and cultures by researching in books or on the internet. What values do they share with different belief systems? What is meant by the 'diversity' of the UK, and what is the history of this diversity? The easiest way for them to start is to talk to the people around them, to ask about their beliefs and views on different issues.

Find out more

www.bbc.co.uk/schools/religion/ – Find out about the beliefs and customs of different religions, using the BBC's resources for schools.

www.diversityanddialogue.org.uk – Diversity and Dialogue is an education project, from the Citizenship Foundation, using local and global issues to build understanding between young people of different faiths and backgrounds.

<table>
<tr><td>

3</td><td>

Raise awareness – yours and others'</td></tr>
</table>

As the saying goes, knowledge is power. Before students start trying to bring about change, they need to know as much as possible about their issue so that they can make an informed decision about the most effective course of action. On top of that, unless they can really explain the problem, and defend their ideas for change, they will find it hard to win the help and support that they need. They have to convince others that their understanding is right, and show them why. The more people who know about a problem, the more public opinion shifts, the greater the pressure is on those who have the power to make a change.

So, your students' first challenge is to find out as much as they can. There are many different ways of letting other people know what they find. Most of the actions in this chapter are based around research and writing, and so work well as lesson or homework activities.

Find out as much as you can

Your students may have identified a problem but need to find out more to know how they can make a difference. Alternatively, they might think there is an obvious change to be made, but a closer look can reveal a more complicated picture. Either way, they need to find out more. Do people disagree on the scale of the problem, or exactly what the problem is? What are the options for change? What impact do students think these different actions will have, and how would those involved feel about the different outcomes? What do the people who are against change think – might their view have any worth? What is the history of the problem? Has anyone tried to make a change before, and with what success?

The first, and easiest, way for students to find out more is to talk to people. Ask students in pairs to write down everything they know about their issue and feed it back to the class. Or set homework to interview a parent or a peer. What does their chosen interviewee know about the problem and where they could find out more? What might their interviewee's agenda or bias be?

On school and local issues, this process of information collection is really important. Students have the advantage of being able to talk directly to the people who are involved or who will be affected by a change. Before taking action they should try to talk to as many of these different groups as possible. For example, if they think the arrangements at break-time should be changed, they should consult with their classmates and friends, as well as both younger and older students, who might feel differently. They could find out how their parents feel and what the staff who monitor break-time think. Ask students to put together and trial a questionnaire or key questions for an interview. Are their questions neutral? Have they thought about how they will record the responses?

Inviting a subject specialist to come and talk in school provides students with the opportunity to find out more directly from someone with in-depth knowledge. See the 'Find out more' section for organizations that offer guest speakers.

To plan how to make a difference beyond their school or immediate community, students will need to get at least some of their information second hand. The media is the obvious way of finding out about the wider world, though they may need guidance on how to select and value information they find there.

First, what is the best source of information on their issue? Different newspaper and news programmes use different criteria to select their 'news'. Students may know to look in local newspapers and on local news programmes for local issues, and in national newspapers for news that affects, or is of interest to, the whole country. They may not know that national newspapers do not always give great coverage of international issues. You could point interested students to the One World or Panos websites. Where do students think they are most likely to find the news they are looking for?

Secondly, once they have selected a news item, what value should they place on the information in it? Can students work out how the information has been biased or spun? There are lots of different clues they can look at. A good start is to identify the number of statements of fact in relation to statements of opinion. 'The Minister answered questions at 3.45 p.m.' is clearly a statement of fact (though it may be inaccurate), while 'The Minister's first answer was weak' is opinion. If students are using an article from a newspaper, where in the paper does it come from? If it is in the 'editorial' section or in a column which appears every week, it may well be opinion. What is the style of writing? Is it gossipy and informal? Tabloid newspapers (like the *Sun* and the *Mirror*) often write like this. Broadsheet news-papers (like the *Guardian* and *The Times*) tend to write more in-depth articles, with statements backed up with details. Do students know of other examples or already have impressions of these different types of paper? It is worth emphasizing that both tabloids and broadsheets can be biased, and just being written in complicated language doesn't make information reliable – it is always worth checking other sources.

You could point out that even photographs can be used to give dif-ferent messages depending on what is included in the image, when the picture is taken and the caption written with the photograph. It is also possible to re-work photographs digitally.

Students can look out for newspaper articles and radio and tele-vision programmes at home, but the most easily accessible resource for research, particularly at school, is the internet. However, students need to learn to be even more discerning when using this media. Have they heard of the Press Complaints Commission? This body ensures that newspapers and magazines follow codes of practice, including not publishing inaccurate or misleading material. For television the BBC has its own regulations, and other channels are monitored by the Independent Television Commission. What about the internet?

What do students think the advantages are of having no regula-tion? Certainly, the internet is very democratic because anyone can have their say, not just a small group of people. What about the dis-advantages? There is no one removing articles that are offensive, dangerous or untrue. So users of the internet have to learn to do this for themselves. As with other media sources, students will have to consider the quality and bias of the information they find, but to help them do this they first need to find out where it comes from. For tips for students on how to get the most out of the internet, see 'How can I safely and effectively use the internet?', p. 66.

Find out more

http://news.bbc.co.uk/cbbcnews – The Newsround website, the BBC news programme for young people.

www.actionaid.org.uk – Action Aid coordinates a team of teachers, who can visit your school to talk about development issues.

www.amnesty.org.uk – Amnesty International offers speakers for schools on human rights.

www.bbc.co.uk – Up-to-date news and background on topical issues.

www.climate-speakers.org.uk – Find a speaker on climate change for your school or group.

www.globaldimension.org.uk – This website includes a 'Speaker Service' database, listing organizations which provide visiting speakers. These include some of the websites listed here, and more.

www.oneworld.net, www.panos.org.uk – Two sources of global news, with a focus on development issues.

www.onlinenewspapers.com – This site allows you to select different countries around the world, and links you to the websites of newspapers there.

www.oxfam.org.uk – Oxfam can arrange a trained volunteer to visit your school to raise awareness of the issues surrounding global poverty and what teachers and students can do to make a difference.

www.redcross.org.uk – The British Red Cross provides 'Ten Minute Briefings' for teachers, summarizing important issues in the news, and 'News Think!', a look at the stories behind recent headlines, with ideas for further exploration.

www.vso.org.uk – Voluntary Service Overseas (VSO) runs a register of Global Educators, professionals who have experience of living and working around the world, and are trained in sharing this experience.

Tell someone

Public opinion, what people on the street think, is very important to all decision makers, for example, politicians, heads of companies and even head teachers! Why do students think that is? Students may not believe it, but changing public opinion isn't all about what is in the media; it starts with them. All they have got to do is tell the people around them. What advantage do students think they have when spreading a message to their friends and family? Are they more likely to listen to a friend or a stranger about a given issue? Whose opinion do they value?

Challenge students to tell another member of the class what they think needs to be changed, and convince them that they are right, using the information they have researched. Or ask every student to pledge that they will tell someone that week.

Telling those around you can help you gain their practical support as well as their agreement with your views. Spreading the message to many people, and starting to change public opinion, can put pressure on those in power. Telling the right person can also have a more direct impact, if students tell someone in a position of political power they are lobbying (see Chapter 4). But it is not just politicians who have the power to make a change. If students tell their friends about the difference they can make through what they buy, their friends might also start considering how to use their consumer power. Or perhaps, by explaining the problems associated with increasing carbon dioxide emissions, they can get their parents thinking about ways to save energy at home.

As well as raising awareness in person, students can get their message across to other individuals in other ways: writing a letter, making a phone call or sending an email (see Chapter 4).

Advertise

Students may want to aim at a larger audience than the friends and family they can tell individually. Companies use words and images on advertisements to persuade us to buy their products or services. However, adverts are not limited to use for commercial profit; students could use them to raise awareness about their cause or issue.

Where do your students commonly see adverts? Would any of these methods of advertising work for their cause or be logistically possible? Could they hand out flyers at school? If there is a school newspaper or magazine, could they approach the editor and place an advert there? Posters are a good way of catching attention and raising interest, though students should be aware that putting up posters on public or private property without permission, fly-posting, is illegal.

Ask students to bring in an advert from a newspaper or magazine that they think is really effective. What makes them want to read it and remember the information on it? Adverts can be funny or shocking, or include a question or puzzle to get people thinking. They also try to make the customer think that by buying a product, they will be a better or more attractive person. It might not be accurate to tell people that by learning more about an issue they will become better-looking. But how do students think they can show that the issue being advertised is relevant to people's lives?

Big companies and big charities use famous people to endorse their message. Why do students think this works as an advertising strategy?

Are there members of the school or local community who carry particular sway and could get involved in an advertising campaign?

Students need to think carefully about who they are targeting and what will appeal to their audience. They could also consider the following elements when designing their advert:

◆ Slogan or title – short, catchy and attention grabbing;
◆ Colour and fonts – bold and clear to get people reading;
◆ Pictures – a very effective way of communicating lots of information quickly, and a good way to break up text;
◆ Key facts – to back up their point, explaining what the problem is and why they think it needs changing;
◆ Contact details or a website – so that people can find out more.

Find out more

www.makepovertyhistory.org – Make Poverty History is a really effective awareness-raising campaign, which has used advertising as well as other strategies.

Write an article

Another way of using the media to target a wide audience is through an article in a paper or magazine. It is an opportunity for students to explain their concerns in-depth. They could write for the school paper, and there may also be publications aimed specifically at young people in the area – do students know of any?

For homework students could contact the editor of the school magazine, or find out who they would need to send an article to. In class, support them to use the research they have done to write about their issue. Is there a quote or dramatic fact or story that they can use at the start to draw the reader in? They will need a bold, clear title and pictures if possible. Can they give examples, or make comparisons that will help readers relate what they are talking about to their own experience? What facts will they need to give to back up their opinion?

Find out more

www.citizenshipfoundation.org.uk – The Citizenship Foundation runs a National Political Journalism competition.
www.earthfocus.org – An environmental magazine written by young people for young people.

<u>**Sharks – The Mistake of Mankind**</u>

It is a commonly known fact that sharks are among the most dangerous animals on Earth. They are vicious, spiteful and adore to devour humans.

It is a rarely known fact that this is a total misconception. Sharks are creatures that hate to mingle with the dangerous humans of the land. Only bad publicity has turned these animals into monstrous creatures of the deep.

Children from the youngest age are led to thinking that sharks are dangerous creatures to be feared and hated. Films such as Finding Nemo and Shark Tale advertise the danger of sharks and persuade viewers that sharks are horrible and mean.

Older children's views of sharks are reinforced by horror movies such as JAWS and by reading newspapers and magazines; you often find a story of a man-eating shark slaughtering a surfer.

In fact, of the more than four hundred and fifty species of shark, few are actually dangerous to humans. The term 'shark - attack' sounds as though sharks viciously attack people when in reality, most shark bites are mistakes.

Instead, humans deliberately prey on sharks. The famous shark fin soup is a delicacy in Asia, but there is horror behind it. Sharks are caught, 'finned', and then dumped back into the sea. Most of the shark is wasted, and some shark species are threatened by this horrible practice.

Sharks are fascinating, there is so much interesting to learn about them. Shark's skin is not made of scales like fish, but of 'denticles', which are a bit like teeth and make the skin extra tough. Some of the largest types of sharks, such as whale sharks, only eat plankton. Two-thirds of a shark's brain is used for its sharpest sense – smell.

I strongly believe that sharks are not the monsters that many people think they are. If only we could leave them alone.

By Antoinette Duplay

Figure 3.1   *Name*: Antoinette Duplay.
What I think needs changing: Peoples' negative view of sharks.
What change action I took: Wrote an article and submitted it to a local magazine.

Give a speech or talk

Giving a speech or talk is a further possible action that allows students to get their message across to a number of people at once. It is a method that allows them to show their passion and determination more personally than in writing, and unlike writing an article, they have a captive audience – if they can keep their attention! Point out to students that people with power often use public speaking as a way of touching people's hearts as well as their minds. For example the film *An Inconvenient Truth* is a recording of the American politician Al Gore delivering a speech on climate change. Can students think of other examples?

At school there are lots of opportunities for students to speak to their peers. Can they have a few minutes in registration or in a lesson that relates to their issue? Teachers can support a class or smaller group to develop an assembly for the year or even the whole school.

Before they start writing, ask students to think about what makes a good speech. Can they remember going to any particularly good presentations? What stood out for them? You could play students a famous speech, or if that is not possible, give them transcripts, and ask them what makes it effective. Try the 'I have a dream' speech by Martin Luther King, or one of Winston Churchill's 1940s speeches. Students should think carefully about both what they are going to say and how they are going to put it across to the audience. Can they think of ways of keeping the audience engaged? Could they use props and pictures to illustrate what they are saying – or a projection of their key points?

It can help to give students the opportunity to practise, perhaps in front of a smaller audience like their class. They should remember to speak clearly, slowly and audibly and to keep their speech short and to the point. It may help to keep their audience's attention if they vary their tone and how loudly they talk. Encourage them not to use the written version of the talk, because they will end up looking down at it instead of looking out at the audience.

Organize an event

If students are after a more challenging approach to raising aware-ness (this is one they certainly can't complete in lesson time), they could plan and run their own event. This can work particularly well for a small group of students who want to commit some time to the project.

The aim is to get people who might be interested into one place, so that students can then get their ideas across to them. To attract their audience, students could combine their message with some form of entertainment. Can they think of examples of events like this?

When planning their event, students should consider what skills and resources they have to offer. For example, if they are confident artists or musicians, could they organize an exhibition or concert? Also important to consider is how they will link the event to their issue. Could they give a short introductory talk? Or use it as an opportunity to display posters and distribute flyers? Can they get the school or local press to cover the event, so that the message goes out beyond those people who attend (see 'How can I let the media know about my lobbying action?', p. 89). Encourage students to think about how they are going to publicize the event. Have they considered posters and flyers, announcements in assembly and in class, the school newspaper, websites, email, and of course, word of mouth (see 'Advertise', p. 61)?

If they charge for entry, students could combine raising awareness with fund-raising for their chosen cause (see Chapter 6).

Find out more

www.g-nation.co.uk – Giving Nation has lots of ideas about good awareness and fund-raising events, and also how to publicize them.

Use the internet to get your message across

The internet allows students to reach far more people than they ever could before. They don't have to have their ideas approved by the editor of a newspaper or limit themselves to an audience the size of a school hall. They can make their ideas available for anyone to see, instantaneously. There are a number of quick and easy ways to post information on the internet, and with a bit of research on how to set them up (see 'Find out more'), these are change actions students can make, or learn the skills to make, in class.

Students can join an online forum, such as a discussion board, discussion group or a message group (see 'How can I safely and effectively use the internet?', p. 66). There are a huge number of sites where they may be able to find a discussion on the issue they want to see changed. If students have a lot to say on an issue, they could start a 'blog'. 'Blog' is short for weblog, and 'blogging' is posting diary-like pages to a website. 'Bloggers' post their most recent findings and

How can I safely and effectively use the internet?

The internet allows us to access information and contact people we never would have before. This makes it an amazing resource, but because it is unregulated it can also be dangerous. It is possible to access potentially harmful material like pornography and racist writing. It is also possible to be contacted by people you may not want contact with, and for people to get access to information about you.

There is a lot of advice available on how to use the internet safely. Do not open emails or files from people you don't know or trust. If you find web material that makes you uncomfortable, just close it down. If you find yourself in a conversation that makes you uncomfortable, or you receive threatening messages, leave the website. Don't respond to messages you are unhappy about, and talk to an adult, especially if such messages are to your personal email. Never give out personal information (your last name, your phone number, where you live, where you go to school, your picture), or agree actually to meet anyone you have met online, without first asking your parents.

You also have responsibilities when you use the internet. Do not post offensive comments or untrue information. Do not send unpleasant or aggressive messages via email, in chat rooms or in discussion groups. It is also a good idea to avoid writing in capital letters; it's a bit like shouting.

There are also a number of steps you can take to help ensure that information you find on the internet is reliable. You will need to do some detective work:

♦ Start by being really specific in choosing the key words you put into your search engine. This will help you get information that matches what you want to read about. If you can, include the name of a relevant organization, a place or a person, to narrow the search.

♦ When you have found a choice of pages, look at the URL (the web address).

  □ If it has a personal name in it (e.g. A.N. Other, often followed by ~ or per cent) this means it is probably a personal website. You will need to do some research on the author. You could try putting their name into a search engine to see what comes up – though remember to be critical of what you read about them too!

□ Look at the last part of the URL, this tells you a lot about the organization it comes from (in the UK, .org for not-for-profit organizations such as charities, .gov for government, and .ac for universities).

□ The publisher of a page is usually the individual or organization operating the 'server' computer from which the page is issued (you normally find it between the *http://* and the first /). Does it come from an organization you have heard of? One that works in the area you are trying to find out about?

◆ Look on the webpage itself to see if you can find out who wrote it. Does the author have good qualifications for writing on this issue? Look for links that say things like 'About us' and 'Background'.

◆ Is the webpage dated? Is the information recent, or already out-of-date?

◆ You can always work backwards from the page to try and find out more. There may be a link to the homepage, or you can remove the last part of the web address, back to the last /, and see what you can find on that page.

◆ Can you see links and references to other sources that you know are reliable? You can research this further at http://alexa.com. If you type your website URL into the search box, it will give you information about how many other websites link to the website you are interested in, as well as giving you an idea of the number of people who visit it. It will also give you details about the organization that owns that domain name. Another way of finding out which websites link to a particular site is to type 'link:' into Google, and then straight afterwards, with no gap, type the URL address. Instead of a normal search, you will then get a search of all the sites that link to the site you put in.

(Continued)

How can I safely and effectively use the internet?—Cont'd

◆ Always try and confirm the information you find by checking that you get the same result from a number of different sources.

Find out more

http://alexa.com – A website that provides information on other websites.

www.allexperts.com – A website that enables you to ask an expert about your issue.

www.askforkids.com – A search engine specifically for young people.

www.blogsafety.com – A website where parents, teenagers, educators and experts can discuss and learn about safe blogging and social networking.

www.getnetwise.org, www.wisekids.org.uk – Websites offering young people, and parents, advice on how to use the internet safely.

www.kidsclick.org – A directory of information created for children by librarians.

---

reflections, just like in a diary, but unlike a diary the most recent entry displays first and it is intended to be read by anyone.

If students want to create their own webpage, a quick way is to set up a 'wiki', which allows anyone (or anyone who has access) to add, edit, or remove content. A wiki is a way of allowing lots of people to work together on a webpage. Wikipedia is the most famous example – an encyclopedia created by thousands of different people with different specialist knowledge.

With a bit more equipment, it is also possible to use the internet to deliver what students say as well as what they write to a wide audience. A podcast is an audio file which is delivered directly over the web, to the computers of those who want to listen to it.

Find out more

http://juicereceiver.sourceforge.net/index.php – Helps you receive and manage podcasts.

www.blogger.com, www.easyjournal.com – Two websites where you can start a free blog.

www.easypodcast.com – Information on how to create a podcast.

www.podcast.net – A directory of podcasts.

www.seedwiki.com – A website where you can create a free wiki.

Wear something to identify yourself with your cause

It is possible for students to raise awareness for their cause without saying or writing anything. Wearing a band around their wrist, a badge or a ribbon identifies them with the associated issue.

What causes have your students heard of that produce badges, ribbons or bands? What message do students think they give to other people by wearing one? Encourage students to think about what they would say if someone asked them why they were wearing a particular badge.

Wearing the band or ribbon of a cause is a quick and easy change action for students to complete – though they will probably need to buy it out of school.

<table>
<tr><td>4</td><td># Lobby – get those with power to make a change</td></tr>
</table>

There are lots of issues on which students will not be able to take direct action because they do not hold the power to make a change. When that is the case, they can learn to be lobbyists to influence those involved in decision making.

Lobbying actions can be used to bring about any kind of change, but the term specifically refers to putting pressure on those who make national decisions and laws. The information in the section 'How is the country run?', p. 72, explains how these kinds of decisions are made in the UK and whom students should contact on what issues. Teachers can use this as a quick reminder for themselves or as an explanation that can be given directly to students.

Find out who else wants to make a difference

Students need to find out what is going on around their issue of concern; what lobbying is already taking place? They will not always have to start from scratch, but can strengthen an existing campaign. If students are exploring and identifying their own change actions, rather than being given a predetermined opportunity to participate, this is an important starting point for them.

What do students think are the advantages of working with others towards a shared goal? In what ways can teamwork be more effective than working alone? What if the goal is to put pressure on someone else? Why is it that companies and elected representatives can easily ignore one person, but cannot usually afford to go against the wishes of large numbers of their consumers or electorate?

A homework task could be to look out for relevant campaigns in the media. Alternatively, they can get immediate information on the internet, searching for organizations they have heard of or using keywords from the issue they are concerned about (see 'How can I safely and effectively use the internet?', p. 66).

Many organizations have a unit specifically for the young people who support them. Students may want to consider joining or supporting a group or campaign on a specific issue (e.g. anti-animal testing or anti-war), or finding a group whose broader beliefs or convictions they agree with. You could encourage students to think about political parties in this context: as groups of individuals with common ideas on what laws should be made, the services that the government should provide, and how the country should behave towards other countries. Point out that they are unlikely to find a party whose policies entirely match their views, but they may find one that matches their general stance. Students can join the Conservative Party and Liberal Democrat Party at any age, and the Labour Party once they are over 15 years of age. There are also youth sections of these parties, which are active in different parts of the country.

Find out more

www.conservativefuture.com – The website for the Conservative movement for under-30s.

www.labour.org.uk/younglabour/ – Young Labour is the youth section of the Labour Party.

www.ldys.org.uk – The website of the Liberal Democrat Youth and Students, the youth wing of the Liberal Democrat Party.

www.youthagainstclimatechange.org – a climate change campaign that aims to reach every student in the UK.

How is the country run?

Understanding how government works and who makes the decisions that affect you will help you understand whom you need to lobby on different issues.

What is central government?

Central government, or the UK government, is the body that has the power to make, and authority to enforce, decisions and laws about how the country should be run. In the UK, the government is divided into three branches: the Judiciary, the group that applies laws through courts and judges; the

Legislature, the part that makes the laws (known also as Parliament); and the Executive, the group that makes the day-to-day decisions, and is headed by the Prime Minister. It is this last part that people usually refer to as 'government'. The UK is a democracy, a system of government in which people have a say in how the country is run. So people over 18 years of age are able to vote for the people who make the laws (the Members of Parliament), which in turn influences who makes up the government.

How does Parliament work?

The UK is divided into areas, called constituencies, 659 in total. All the people in each area can vote for the individual they most want to represent them, from a choice of candidates. The person with the most votes becomes the Member of Parliament, or MP. The MPs meet together in the House of Commons in the Houses of Parliament in London (the building which includes Big Ben). They meet regularly to put forward new laws (or bills), discuss and vote on them, and also to examine the work of the government. Each MP represents all their constituents (the people who live in their constituency), but they are not required to follow what their constituents want them to vote for.

The MPs, generally, though not always, belong to political parties. Parties are groups of people with shared ideals about how the country should be run. When these ideals are broken down to specific ideas on specific issues they are called policies. The three main parties in Britain today are the Labour party, the Conservative party and the Liberal Democrat party. The MPs who do not belong to a party are known as independents.

How are the Prime Minister and government decided on?

The leader of the party to which the most MPs belong becomes the Prime Minister (PM). The PM chooses up to

(Continued)

How is the country run?—Cont'd

95 members of the MPs in his or her party to form the government. They are given different jobs (such as the Minister for Education, the Minister for Health), and they run departments, such as the Foreign and Commonwealth Office (for dealing with relations with other countries) and the Home Office (for immigration, security, police and prisons). About 20 of the most important ministers form the cabinet, which is the core of the government and which makes final decisions about policies and what the government should do in important situations.

As well as leading the cabinet, and being the key government figure in the House of Commons, the PM has other roles including overseeing the operation of the civil service, heading the armed forces and representing the nation in international affairs.

What is the Civil Service?

The Civil Service are the people who help the government to carry out the decisions that they have made, and to provide public services. They administrate and advise government members and government departments. They do not work directly for the government, but for 'the crown'; so, they cannot side with any party and what it stands for.

What stops the government doing anything it wants, once it has the power?

In theory, a government can do anything that it wishes. As long as it is within the law, it does not need to ask anyone's opinion. However, there are mechanisms to stop this happening and to oversee the work of the government. First, and most obviously, if a government does things that lots of people disagree with, at the next election (a maximum of 5 years from the last), the public will vote for different MPs and the government will lose power.

Secondly, MPs who do not agree with a proposed law can vote against it. The MPs who are not in the party that makes up the government regularly vote against government proposals. The party with the second largest number of MPs is called the Opposition party, and their leader appoints an MP to 'shadow' each member of the cabinet and question what they do. The MPs from the party in power also do not have to vote for a government proposal if they disagree with it. This is common among 'back-benchers', MPs that hold no particular role in their party. However, MPs get in trouble if they vote against their party too often. Each party has a 'whip', an MP whose job it is to keep the party in order. If MPs fail to follow the 'whip', they risk not being promoted or having to resign from the party.

A further important check on the government is the House of Lords, also part of Parliament. The people in the House of Lords, called peers, are not elected. They inherit the title through their family or are appointed for their lifetime. They are there to monitor what the House of Commons does. Before a law can be passed, the House of Lords must agree with it, and if they don't they can send it back to the House of Commons for them to consider it again. In this way, they can delay a law by up to a year, though they cannot stop it altogether.

The place of the House of Lords in the making of laws is controversial. Supporters say that it offers an important check to decision making in the House of Commons. Opponents say that allowing unelected individuals to have a say in law making is not democratic. In 1999, all but 92 of the 750 peers who inherited their title lost their right to vote. A minority of peers are now selected by an independent body rather than by the Prime Minister. The House of Lords is undergoing reform, though the debate over how far these changes should go continues.

Finally, before a bill becomes a law the Queen has to agree to it. Theoretically, she could refuse to agree to a law, but in practice she always does, and in fact she no longer gives her agreement personally.

What is local government?

While Parliament and central government make laws and decisions that affect the whole country, there are thousands of

(*Continued*)

How is the country run?—Cont'd

local decisions that it would be impossible and impractical for MPs to make. In every region there are choices to be made about how best to provide services the government has promised and how to implement laws that have been passed. Local governments, also called councils or local authorities, make these local decisions. They deal with providing education, services for the vulnerable (like care for older people and disabled people), homes for those on low income and services for the whole population such as museums, libraries, parks and sports centres. They also regulate pubs, clubs, markets and new buildings, and enforce rules on parking and dumping.

Just like MPs, members of local government, often called councillors, are elected by the public, usually every four years. They usually have other jobs and do not get paid for the work they do. Local government can be confusing because there is no single system in the UK. The official and unofficial names given to local government bodies and the roles they carry out vary from region to region. They include county, district, city, borough, town and parish councils, and unitary authorities. London has its own form of local government, the Greater London Authority. You can find out what type of local government representatives you have and what they are responsible for by entering your postcode at www.writetothem.com.

What is devolution?

Since 1997 government has taken steps to spread the decision-making power out from London, a process called 'devolution'. There is now a Parliament in Scotland which can make laws in certain areas such as health, education, the environment and policing. Assemblies in Wales and Northern Ireland cannot make their own laws but decide how laws made in Parliament in London should be applied.

What is the European Parliament?

After 50 million civilians died in World War II, European countries started to think about working together, to try and prevent war in the future. One of the main ways they did this was allowing products to be traded from country to country and people to move freely between countries. This was known originally as the European Economic Community, but since then has undergone many changes. It is now called the European Union (EU) and has 27 member countries. Over-18s in the UK can vote for Members of the European Parliament (MEPs). The MEPs meet in Strasbourg in France, and Brussels in Belgium, to debate and vote on European laws.

The following summary should help you understand whom you need to contact with different issues:

◆ For issues relating to European law, contact your MEP;
◆ For issues relating to national law, decisions that affect the whole country, or relations between Britain and other countries, contact your local MP;
◆ For issues relating to local services such as schools, social services, local transport, roads, libraries, planning or rubbish collection, contact one of your local government representatives.

Find out more

http://europa.eu – The portal site of the EU, where you can find out more about the union and its member countries – includes pages aimed at young people.

www.theyworkforyou.com – Lets you know what your MP is doing in his or her role as your representative.

www.upmystreet.com/commons/l/ – This parliamentary website allows you to search by postcode to find out who your MP is.

www.writetothem.com – This website gives you details of your local, national and EU representatives. It enables you to send them a letter via email, and gives lots of good advice about the most effective way of getting your point across to them.

Write a letter

One way of introducing this change action is to consider the value of a letter. Why can letters still be an important tool in an age of quick hi-tech communication? Why not just send an email? Letters have always been valued because they are personal, even carrying the sender's own seal or signature. In writing you put time and even a bit of yourself into the letter, unlike more anonymous emailing. Not only that, but letters sit on the receiver's desk, not in their inbox, and can be less easily lost or ignored.

The first thing students need to do is to decide who it would be most effective to send their letter to. They need to consider who has the power to make the change they want. They may know immediately that they need to target an individual (e.g. the headteacher about the school reward system), or a particular company (e.g. a supermarket that doesn't stock MSC-certified fish).

However, it is not always easy to know who could make the difference. For example, if students are unhappy that the local buses are often late, they may quickly come up with the idea of writing to the local bus company. However, it could also be a good idea to write to their local council, who fund the bus system. Because local councils and central government are involved in making many decisions that affect them, students may well need to understand how power is distributed before they can work out whom they need to contact (see 'How is the country run?', p. 72).

Emphasize that it is worth students finding a specific person to write to. Why do students think this is? A letter addressed to an individual is much more likely to get to the right place than a letter addressed to an organization (e.g. a bank) or even to a position (e.g. the bank manager). It can be annoying when people get your name or details wrong, and students want to look as professional as possible.

A good ICT task is tracking down a name and address to write to. Students can try looking on the organization's website for a 'Contact us' section, and for the details of the Head of Customer Services, or the Manager or Director. Alternatively, from home, students can use the phone book, and ring to ask for the name of the person they should write to.

If students want to raise awareness for their cause, they could consider writing an 'open letter', addressed to an individual, but published in a magazine or newspaper.

Next, students need to think about the content of their letters. The guidelines on p. 80 could be copied or displayed to help them.

Students may have taken part in, or heard about, pre-written letter or postcard campaigns. This is an easier approach than writing their own, and can be an easy change action to complete. But how effective a lobbying action do students think it is? Which do they think is more likely to go in the bin: one of 300 identical letters, or an individual letter expressing their personal views? Are they happy to sign up to all the views expressed in the pre-written letter? Writing their own letter shows they care enough to take the time to write, rather than just cutting and pasting.

Find out more

www.amnesty.org/campaign/letter-guide.html – A guide to letter writing on human rights issues, including sample letters.

---

21 Rue du St-Genis
Geneva
28th September 2007

Mr. Hunt
Headteacher
International School of St-Genis

Dear Mr. Hunt

I am a year 8 student and I am writing to you about the current situation of the school lunch queue. I am afraid to tell you that the lunch queue needs serious action. Every day, students have to wait in long lines just to have lunch. People push each other and accidents happen. The system needs to be changed.

I have suggestions on how to solve some of the problems. I think that the line should be divided into bigger students and younger students. I think that the teachers should supervise and I think the lunch card system should be stopped to improve the speed.

Thank you for reading this letter, I hope you will consider my suggestions.

Yours sincerely,

Miguel J Pagdilao

Figure 4.1 *Name*: Miguel Pagdilao.
What I think needs changing: The lunch-queue system at school.
The change action I took: Wrote a letter to the headteacher.

How to make my letter professional

Letter writing etiquette

- Put your address and the date in the top right hand corner of the page;
- Put the name and the address of the person you are writing to below your address, but on the left-hand side;
- Leave a space and write 'Dear' and then their title and surname;
- Sign off your letter 'Yours sincerely,' if you have started it with their name, or 'Yours faithfully,' if you started 'Dear Sir or Madam'. If the letter is typed (which is clearer and smarter), leave space to sign the letter and then type your name – remember to sign it before you send it.

In the main part of the letter there are fewer rules, but you should think about the following points to make yourself clear

- It is helpful for the person reading it if you open by explaining exactly why you are writing. For example, you might write 'I am writing to you regarding the sale of products tested on animals in your shop';
- Then explain who you are and why you are interested in writing. You could give details like your age and the school you go to, and then explain why you feel strongly about your cause. Include facts and details to support your case. For example you could write 'I'm 14 and I live in Norwich. I use your shop regularly. However, I believe strongly in the rights of animals, and was disappointed to find that your shop stocks products tested on animals. These products include . . .';
- State clearly what you would like the addressee to do. No one likes to receive a letter that is all complaints and no constructive path for what can be changed. For example, you could write 'I am writing to ask you to consider discontinuing the brands that you sell that are tested on animals';
- You could finish on a new line by saying 'Thank you for taking the time to consider my points', or 'Thank you for taking the time to help me', or 'I look forward to hearing from you'.

Keep the letter brief, no longer than one side of A4. Make sure that it is always polite and clear. You need to make sure that the reader will read to the end and consider your argument. Keep a copy of your letter.

Send an email – join an e-campaign

What do students think are the pros of email? They're obviously quick, global and cheap, and they enable a message to be sent to a lot of people without the author having to leave the house for a stamp or wait for the post to arrive. What about the cons? People can get fed up if their inboxes get clogged with lots of identical anonymous messages. Certainly, annoying someone is one way of getting their attention, but it is not generally the best way of getting them to do what you want. Sending an email is deceptively easy. Remind students not to be fooled into rushing into an email without considering the impact their message will have.

Emails tend to be less formal than letters, but for an effective email, the same rules apply about finding the right person to write to and being polite and clear. The letter writing guide on p. 80 could help students construct their draft.

Speak to someone

Sometimes, the best way to get a message across to someone is to tell them yourself. Why do students think that is? What body language signals do they think they give out when they try to persuade someone in person? What can they pick up about what an issue means to someone else from the way they talk?

Again, the first step is for students to consider whom they need to contact. Meeting someone in person is only likely to be a good option locally, for example, a member of school staff, or the manager of a local shop. Teachers could invite a local councillor or an MP into the classroom to enable students to speak to him or her directly. Alternatively, they can help students prepare for out-of-school meetings. Students will need to arrange the meeting by contacting the person by email, phone or letter, explaining why they want to meet. They will need to consider practical issues like how they will get there, what they should wear, and whether they will need an adult to come with them.

Teachers can help students prepare for the contents as well as the logistics of the meeting. Encourage them to draft an ideal script, answering the following questions:

- Who are they?
- Why did they arrange the meeting?

- Why do they feel so strongly about the issue?
- What do they want the person they are meeting to do about it?

Students could run a 'mock-meeting' with a partner, practising how to respond to unexpected questions and establishing a way forward from the meeting. Remind students to stay calm and polite, and to keep a record of the details of the meeting in case they do not get the outcome they want and need to take further action (see 'How can I follow-up my lobbying action?', p. 83).

One way for students to use all their charm and powers of persuasion but without having to arrange a meeting is to make a short video or DVD. They can then send their campaign video as a personal message to individuals with the power to make a change.

Find out more

www.theyworkforyou.com – Searchable by postcode for your local Member of Parliament (MP). Also gives contact information and the MP's personal website, if one exists, which you can then use to find out when his or her next surgery is.

Sign or start a petition

What do students understand by the term petition? It can help to explain that it is like writing a letter, but then getting lots of other people to sign it. Do students think petition writing is an effective way of lobbying? What are the advantages and disadvantages? Petitions are a quick way of demonstrating that a large number of people support an issue. However, a signature alone does not demonstrate an in-depth understanding of a problem; it only shows that a person cared enough to give up a few seconds of their time.

As with all lobbying actions, students need to think first about who should receive their petition and find the contact details of that person. Secondly, it is important that the letter part of the petition is good. There is no point in having lots of signatures if it is not clear what they're all signing up to support. Use the letter writing guide on p. 80 for students who need help drafting their petition letters.

Class time, form-time or assemblies can provide good slots for students to explain to their peers why they should sign their petition.

How can I follow-up my lobbying action?

Whatever kind of lobbying action you take, if you don't get the response you wanted you will need to follow it up. This means repeating your action or choosing another one to strengthen your campaign.

If you choose to write, email or talk to someone, clearly requesting a response, you may want to contact that individual again. You should remind them that you have contacted them before, giving the date you wrote or spoke to them. This is why it can be a good idea to keep a record of any lobbying action you take, including copies of letters.

If you still do not receive a response from an individual or organization, or are unhappy about the reply you get, there will often be a complaints procedure you can follow (look on the organization's website) or a body that is in charge of regulating what they do.

An ombudsman is a word for an official, or body, that is in charge of addressing complaints reported by an individual citizen. If you have a problem with your local authority, a government department, the health service, an insurance company, a bank, a building society or a legal service, and are not happy with how your complaint was dealt with, you can contact the relevant ombudsman.

Find out more

www.financial-ombudsman.org.uk – The Financial Ombudsman Service.
www.ipcc.gov.uk – The Independent Police Complaints Commission.
www.lgo.org.uk – The Local Government Ombudsman.
www.olso.org – The Office of Legal Service Ombudsman.
www.ombudsman.org.uk – The Parliamentary and Health Service Ombudsman.
www.pcc.org.uk – The Press Complaints Commission.

They could set up a desk in the foyer or corridor as a base to persuade passing students, or be challenged to get a certain number of signatures from family and friends. It is the student's responsibility to make sure that those signing understand what they are signing and who it will be sent to. Students can spend class or homework time designing a petition form with space for name, address and signature. Or they could draft an explanation of why they think people should sign, to be added to the petition form or read to potential signatories.

Finally, students need to think about how to deliver their petition to its intended audience. They could send it through the post. Or they could arrange a meeting to present it to the recipient in person, giving them an opportunity to really explain why the issue is so important to all the undersigned (see section 'Speak to someone', p. 81).

For a quick computer-based change action students could sign an online petition, of which there are a growing number. Lots of petition sites also provide students with the opportunity to create an online petition of their own, with access to huge numbers of signatories.

Find out more

http://petitions.pm.gov.uk – A website where you can sign and create petitions for the Prime Minister.

www.avaaz.org – Avaaz.org is a 'community of global citizens who take action on the major issues facing the world today'. The word Avaaz means voice or song in several languages, and the website allows you to sign petitions on global issues.

www.gopetition.com – A leading international host portal for online petitions.

www.thebigask.com – A visual petition to the government, asking for a strong climate law.

Join an online forum

Online forums allow contributors to express their individual views rather than signing up to a given statement. Through discussion, students can also develop their understanding of an issue. Some forums not only provide the opportunity to persuade other contributors, but also channel students' views straight to decision makers. All students need to do is register to these forums and then log in and join the debate.

Say 'NO' to animal-tested make-up

When people argue that animal testing should be allowed, they say that animals are tested on 'for the good of human beings'. But animals are tested on for more than just finding cures to illnesses. Some companies still test make-up on animals. They torture animals, just so that people can wear lipstick and mascara. Humans should be protecting animals, not hurting them for no good reason.

It is not legal to test make-up on animals in the UK, but it is easy to buy make-up that has been made in other countries where it can be tested on animals. The local chemist stocks some animal-tested make-up. We want to show them that many of their customers find it offensive that they sell these products. There are lots of good non-animal-tested make-up they could sell instead.

Our aim is to collect as many signatures as possible, and then give this petition to the manager of the chemist. Sign here, and show that you think that animal testing, and selling animal-tested products is unacceptable.

SHOW YOU CARE, it will only take a minute.

Name	Address	Signature

Figure 4.2 *Name*: Imogen Aitken and Aura Viale.
What we think needs changing: Animals being used to test make-up.
The change action we took: Made a petition to send to the local chemist that stocks animal-tested make-up.

Find out more

www.bigvote.org.uk – 'I'm a councillor, get me out of here' is a project that allows students to talk to their local councillor over the internet during local democracy week, in October.

www.headsup.org.uk – Heads up is an online debating space for under-18s to share their views on political issues and events. It's a space politicians can use to consult with young people.

Boycott

An interesting way to get students thinking about boycotts is to explore the origin of the word. Ask students to give a definition and ideas of where the term came from.

It is thought to have entered the English language in the 1880s in Ireland, when Captain Charles Boycott, who ran an Earl's estate, responded to tenants' demands to reduce their rents by throwing them off the land. Everyone in the area refused to deal with the businessman, whether that meant stopping trading with him, not delivering post or stopping work for him – the first boycott was organized. Eventually, Captain Boycott left his job. The word is now used to refer to a refusal to deal with any organization or country as a protest against its actions or policy.

Can students think of examples of boycotts that they have heard about or have taken part in? What does a boycott do, other than stop the boycotter buying or doing something they might want? Students may want to refer back to the story of Captain Boycott to explain how boycotts work. In the case of companies, if enough people boycott their food or film, they make less money. To improve sales, their overall aim, they may consider making the changes the boycotters want.

Can students think of any problems with boycotting as an action for change? Large companies will not immediately feel the impact of a small-scale boycott. One way students can make their boycott more effective is by writing to the company involved explaining why they are boycotting its products and why. On the other hand, if the boycott does have a financial impact, the outcomes may be unexpected. Critics of the use of boycotts say that if the company loses out it will reduce production and make workers unemployed. If, for example, students are campaigning to improve working conditions for those employed in the company this isn't what they want!

As well as discussing the use and effectiveness of boycotting as a change action, teachers can use class time to enable groups to find out more about current boycotts. Students could carry out internet research on a boycott to present to the class, or choose a boycott they would like to be involved in and explain why.

Find out more

www.ethicalconsumer.org – The website of the *Ethical Consumer* magazine, with information on boycotts of companies and countries and the reasons behind them.

Go to a demonstration

First, here is a quick definition of some terms which are often used interchangeably to describe a large number of people getting together to put their point across. A rally is a gathering of people for a meeting. It could also be called a public meeting, and will usually have speakers talking about their experiences and ideas. A march, as the term implies, is when the gathering moves! If the meeting or march is aimed at protesting or demonstrating opposition to something, it can also be called a demonstration.

Attending or even organizing one of these activities (for ease, grouped as demonstrations) is obviously not a quick classroom action for change. However, to understand the scope of lobbying actions, students need to learn about demonstrations. Consider discussing a demonstration students have seen locally or in the media. Have any of your students attended a demonstration? Alternatively, students could interview their parents and record an older generation's experiences of demonstrating.

Whatever the context, ask students to think about whether demonstrations are effective lobbying actions? Draw them to consider the clear and visible message a demonstration gives to those with power. Demonstrations can be extremely motivating and upbeat events. They show all those involved how many other people there are who want to make a difference, and what they can achieve if they work together. Demonstrations can also raise awareness for a cause; it is not just the individual or organization with power to make a change that will see it. Lots of members of the public will hear about the demonstration on the news or bump into it on their street, and it may get them thinking. If the demonstration is large and causes disruption, it can add the lobbying pressure of onlookers, who want things to return to normal, to that of participants.

What do students think makes an effective demonstrator? If they carry banners or placards with their key messages and make noise, for example, by chanting, they will attract attention to their demonstration. Emphasize that it is important to maintain this positive atmosphere in demonstrations. They are not an outlet for frustration about an issue. Getting aggressive towards others or damaging property is illegal whatever the cause might be.

Class teachers and school leaders can feel uncomfortable about students wishing to take part in 'political' activity. This is particularly the case for actions like demonstrations that can be seen as disruptive and are highly visible. Awkward questions arise, such as 'Does involvement of our students mean that the school itself is seen to be supporting/opposing the issue?'; 'If students are allowed to demonstrate on one issue, shouldn't they be allowed to demonstrate on other issues they might choose?' Does your school have a position on whether it would ever be acceptable for students to miss school to attend a demonstration? Is this determined by the issue or nature of the demonstration? What would the reaction be to students organizing a demonstration at school? Would that position change if it were a demonstration about an internal issue?

If it is appropriate and logistically possible, and you have a group of committed and determined students, you could support them to stage a small demonstration at school. There are a number of important issues they will need to consider. When and where will it have the most impact? Can it relate physically to the issue they are demonstrating about, or take place at a significant time or on a particular day? Once people are there, how are they going to organize them? They will need to have a clear plan of what they want people to do, and nominate clearly identifiable helpers to guide people. Would it be helpful to have leaflets to distribute to other students to let them know what the demonstration is about? Students will also need to consider the best way to advertise their demonstration so that they get as much support as they can. Have they thought about getting the media involved (see 'How can I let the media know about my lobbying action?' on p. 89), or putting up posters around the school (see section 'Advertise', p. 61). Importantly, if they are planning a march or procession on public property, they are legally obliged to notify the police (under Public Order Act 1986). They will need to give a minimum of six days' notice or they could be fined.

How can I let the media know about my lobbying action?

If you can get a newspaper, radio station, internet site, magazine or TV news programme interested in your petition-sending, boycott, or rally you can increase the impact of your actions in a number of ways.

First, if you are organizing a demonstration and you use the media to inform people about when and where it will be, and why it is being held, you may get more support on that day. Secondly, by getting your lobbying action into the media, you are making lots of people aware that you are asking a decision maker to make a change. If that person doesn't want to do it, they have got to tell all those people who are now aware of what is happening, as well as you. Not all of the people who hear about your actions will agree with you or would have bothered to support you, but they might not be impressed by the MP's or company-director's response. People in power do not want to look bad in front of a large number of their electorate or customers. So by letting more people know about what you are doing you are increasing the pressure on decision makers. Finally, by getting your issue into the media, you raise awareness of your issue and may encourage more people to take action themselves.

Before you contact a journalist, you need to think about what kind of media would get your message across best, and what kind of programme or publication is going to be interested in what you are doing. Think about your school or parish newsletter, or local paper, radio station or news programme. They often have more time for local issues than national papers, radio and television; though you should think about contacting these if you think you have a really exceptional story. Track down the name and details of the specific person you should contact. Find out who writes about issues like this on the school magazine and talk to them personally, or phone or email the newspaper or radio station.

Next, you need to prepare a press or media release. This is a document that lets the media know everything they

(*Continued*)

How can I let the media know about my lobbying action?—Cont'd

might want to know about what you are doing, in a form that is helpful to them and that they are therefore more likely to use.

Think about the following:

- Make the heading bold and the opening interesting;
- The most important questions to answer are: who, what, why, where and when? These points should go as near the start as possible;
- Keep it short, clear and neat. No longer than one side of A4 and preferably typed;
- Put a date on your release, and the date when you are happy for it to be used;
- If you can, include a good quote from yourself or someone else involved in the action, explaining the importance of what you are doing;
- Include your name and an easy way to contact you (such as a mobile number), so they can contact you if they have any questions.

Find out more

http://web.amnesty.org/pages/campaigning-manual-eng – Amnesty International's manual on effective campaigning, including a section on media and publicity.

Go on strike

A strike, or collective stopping of work, is a traditional way of protesting about workplace issues such as poor conditions or low pay. More recently, students in schools and universities have taken part in strikes (in this case stopping learning) to demonstrate concern about a particular issue, for example, as an anti-war statement.

Like demonstrations, striking is not an action for change that fits easily into lesson time! However, students can be given the opportunity to reflect on the use of striking and its role in the UK's history of industrial action. As part of an exploration of possible lobbying actions, or following media coverage of a strike locally or internationally, encourage students to discuss the use of striking. Why is striking in the workplace an effective way of getting the attention of employers? Why can't employers afford for their workers to strike for long? Why do we hear about it more when postal workers strike as opposed to office workers? Why might it be good for the postal workers that it is covered so much in the media?

What do students know about the practicalities of striking? For example, do they think that employees are allowed to strike or not? Can people lose their jobs for striking? This is a good point to introduce the idea of trade unions (see 'What is a trade union?', below). It is not legal to fire an employee in the UK for taking part in a strike if it is official, that is, organized by a trade union.

What is a trade union?

Trade unions are societies of workers. Workers normally join a trade union of other people who do similar work. For example, there are unions for actors and others for teachers. Trade union members work together to protect and improve their working conditions. If a member is treated unfairly by their employer the trade union will support them, in return for their support for other workers.

It is the law in the UK that companies allow their workers to join trade unions, and to take part in action, including strikes, organized by their unions. You cannot be sacked for this. This is not always the case in developing countries; workers in some areas and industries are prevented from joining or forming trade unions, sometimes by violent means.

Find out more

www.nusonline.co.uk – The NUS, National Union of Students, is a union for college and university students.
www.nut.org.uk – The NUT, National Union of Teachers, is one of the unions teachers can join.
w ww.unison.org.uk – The website of UNISON, the UK's biggest trade union. It is a union for people working to provide public services.

What do students think physically happens at a strike? Normally a strike is combined with a demonstration which workers take part in to raise awareness of why the strike is taking place. Those on strike may also picket: they stand outside work and try and prevent any non-striking colleagues from going to work. Why do students think they do this? It is also possible to picket buildings other than workplaces, such as shops. People are free to picket peacefully, as long as they do not cause an obstruction, or behave in a way that threatens or intimidates others.

Finish the discussion by asking students to consider the differences between workplace and classroom strikes. Stopping their own learning will not have an immediate impact on other people or the economy, so how could it work as a lobbying action? You could allow groups of committed campaigners among your students to use a lesson's strike as a form of demonstration.

5

Get to a position of more power for change

Some people, through a position, post or job, hold more power to make changes than others. Traditionally, young people have been viewed as low on the power-ladder: they cannot yet vote in local and general elections, the most obvious form of democratic participation, and many decisions that affect them are made by their families or the state. However, this does not mean that they can't get themselves, or someone they believe in, to a position where they can make a bigger difference. The more they do so, the more experienced and informed they will be to make use of the opportunities that will be available to them when they can work and vote.

Stand for election

Getting elected to a position of greater power may provide students with an opportunity to make a difference on the issues that concern them. In schools, the best way to do this is usually to stand for election to the school council.

School councils are structured and run differently in different schools. Some are made up of representatives elected or selected from year councils; others have members elected directly to the whole-school council. There may be subcommittees whose job it is to carry out different tasks or research different issues (such as bullying, teaching and learning, and catering). Some school councils meet once a week, others once a term, and they vary in the level of power and budget they hold. What they should all have in common is an opportunity for young people to contribute to decision making at school. For advice on setting up or developing a school council see the 'Find out more' section.

Many schools also run elections for the UK Youth Parliament. Members of Youth Parliament (MYPs) hold the position for a year, meeting regularly with other MYPs in the area to discuss the issues they, and those they represent, want to see changed. They meet with local MPs and councillors, organize events, run campaigns, make speeches, hold debates and ensure their views are heard by decision makers. For more information on how your students can get involved, see the UKYP website.

There is also a Youth Eco-Parliament, part of the PRO Europe Congress. Each year students from all over Europe are sent to the Youth Eco-Parliament where they learn and discuss waste management projects with other young people. Unlike the UK Youth Parliament, it is not democratic; delegates are selected by a competition rather than elected. However, it is still an opportunity for students to have their views heard.

Support students who wish to stand for election by helping them understand how the system works and what the post involves. What do they think makes a good representative? Are they organized, good at listening to other people's viewpoints and confident enough to put their ideas forward? If they were elected, what would they want to change? What issues particularly concern them? Those who want to stand will need to draw up a manifesto answering these questions and think about how they will persuade their peers to vote for them.

Once the council is elected, its members need to have time to collect the views of their electorate, and report back on decisions and changes made by the council. Could they be allocated a regular slot in form-time or a room to meet in at break-time? Support students to be more effective councillors by helping them take more than a list of complaints to meetings. You could talk to them about the problems they have identified, and help them formulate clear suggestions and steps for change. If students are frustrated by not being able to make the changes they want, it might be helpful to remind them that while democracy can be slow and inefficient it is a system through which change can be instigated by people like them.

Lessons which introduce the school council or Youth Parliament are good opportunities for pointing out the parallels between school councillors, local government representatives and MPs. Once elected, they all hold the power of the post for a specified time, and may be able to use it to make changes they want to see. If they wish to be re-elected, though, they will need to pay attention to the views of the people who voted for them. The holder of each of these posts represents all the people in their electoral unit (whether that be constituency, ward or year-group), not just the people who voted for them.

However, unlike local and national democratic representatives, school councillors will probably not be members of a political party.

To help students understand the work of Parliament, the Citizenship Foundation runs a National Youth Parliament competition, in which students take on parliamentary roles and create a video of their debate on a mock bill.

Students may be interested to know who can stand for election to positions of political power in the UK (see 'How is the country run?', p. 72). Once they are 18 years of age they can stand to be an MP, provided they are British Citizens, or citizens of a Commonwealth country or the Irish Republic. There are a number of circumstances in which they will not be able to stand, for example, if they are in prison, have been found guilty of cheating in an election or are a civil servant. Candidates for general election need the support of ten voters and must pay a £500 deposit.

At 18 years of age, British citizens, and citizens of the Commonwealth, Irish Republic, or European Union can also stand to be local government representatives, often known as councillors. To do so they must have strong links with the area: have their name on the local electoral register; rent or own land or property in the area; or have lived or worked in the area for the past twelve months.

Since the year 2000 it has also been possible to be put forward by members of the public for a life peerage. Those selected can attend the House of Lords for their lifetime and take part in the debate and voting on British laws that take place there. To be eligible, a nominee must be 21 years of age and a British, Irish or Commonwealth citizen.

Find out more

www.citizenshipfoundation.org.uk – The Citizenship Foundation runs a National Youth Parliament competition.

www.lordsappointments.gov.uk – Get a nomination pack here to appoint someone to the House of Lords.

www.recycle-more.co.uk – Find out about the Youth Eco-Parliament.

www.schoolcouncils.org – School Councils UK is a charity that offers resources, training and support to help schools develop their school councils.

www.ukyouthparliament.org.uk – The website of the UK Youth Parliament.

Lynsey for School Council

Why I would make a good representative

I am Lynsey Macdonald, form 8.1, and I think that I should be elected for the school council because I am organised and I am able to share and express my views clearly.

I would attend every meeting without fail because I am reliable and feel that this is an important quality which representatives need to have.

I am a good listener and I will gladly listen to people's views and feelings attentively.

The things I would work to change if I was elected:

I would try to make it so that you could have a shower after sports and that separate cubicles would be built.

I would campaign to change the packed lunch room or make a new one, with a few more microwaves and larger windows to increase the brightness. I think that the present one is very dark and not a particularly enjoyable place to eat.

I think I would make a good representative so please vote for me and I will try my best to change the points above, and others you have. I think that I can make the school a better place.

Figure 5.1 *Name*: Lynsey MacDonald.
What I think needs changing: The packed-lunch and changing-room facilities at school.
The change action I took: Stood for school council.

Vote

Students don't have to stand for election to get someone they believe will make a difference into power. They can vote for someone else they think will make positive changes.

As with standing for election, school council and Youth Parliament are likely to form students' main experiences of voting at school. This process often mirrors voting in local and general elections, and provides an opportunity for students to develop their understanding of these processes. There will clearly be some differences: instead of a community hall or church, the polling station may be a classroom; instead of the electoral register (the list of registered voters), students may have their name crossed off a school register. It is also unlikely that they will be able to vote by post or proxy in a school election. However, as in a local or general election, students will probably be given a ballot paper on which they put a cross next to their preferred candidate, and a sealed ballot box to put their ballot paper into.

Why do students think it is important to have a 'secret ballot' like this? Did they know that voting is compulsory in some countries, for example, Australia? Why do they think that is? In 2005 only 60 per cent of voters turned out to vote in the UK general elections. Why is this a problem? What is meant by the term 'voter apathy'? What arguments would students use to persuade someone to use their vote? Did they know that in 1800 only men who owned land could vote in the UK, so only one in ten men had the vote, and no women? It was not until 1918 that some women got the vote, and still only those over 30 years of age could vote.

School elections are also a good opportunity to explore the various electoral methods by which the outcome of a vote can be decided. In general and local elections in the UK, and often in school council elections, the elected person is the person with the most votes (a 'first past the post' system). Elections to the European Parliament follow a different system, known as proportional representation, under which the number of seats each party receives is roughly equal to their share of the votes.

To encourage students not just to vote for their friends, time and information needs to be provided to help them make their decision. As with governmental elections, school council elections often have 'campaign' periods during which candidates try to persuade the electorate to vote for them. Each candidate could be allotted time to make a speech at a 'hustings', and space to display their manifesto. Encourage students to question each candidate about issues of particular concern to them, and to consider whether they are trustworthy, reliable and good at putting their point across. Point out that in local and general elections there may be posters, flyers and websites where voters can find out more information, and party members canvassing door-to-door.

To get students further accustomed to voting, and thinking about whom they will vote for when they can, many schools run mock local and general elections. 'Y Vote Mock Elections' provides support and resources for schools to run their own mock elections, and compiles the results nationally.

It may be of interest to older students that they can register their name on the electoral register once they are 16 years of age. They will need to register by the time they are 18 years of age to ensure they can vote as soon as they legally can. British citizens (and Irish and Commonwealth citizens who live in the UK) can vote in general elections unless they are disqualified by being in prison, treated under mental health laws, a member of the House of Lords or recently convicted of corruption in an election. Once they are 18 years of age, students will also be able to vote in local government elections and European Parliamentary elections, provided they are British, Irish, Commonwealth or European Union citizens resident in the UK.

Find out more

www.aboutmyvote.co.uk – Lets you know when elections will be taking place and how to register to vote.

www.electoralcommission.org.uk – The website of the electoral commission, the organization that monitors government elections.

www.mockelections.co.uk – The website of 'Y Vote Mock Elections' which supports schools to run mock elections.

Join a committee or board

Not all groups with power to make changes are elected – sometimes it is possible for students to join a committee or board by putting themselves forward or by being invited.

Do students know of any such opportunities in or outside school? Some schools have non-elected committees which are consulted on issues such as individual discipline cases, or new catering contracts.

What about when they leave school? Many school governors are appointed from the local community, and governing boards are often looking for members at different points in life and with different experience. Once they are 18 years of age, students may also find that they are requested to form part of a jury. Jurors are selected randomly from people on the electoral register, excluding those who have been convicted of a serious criminal offence or been in prison in the last 10 years, and those over 70 years of age. Jury service is compulsory, although it is possible to be excused or allowed to defer for strong work or personal reasons.

Find out more

www.citizenshipfoundation.org.uk – The Citizenship Foundation runs a Bar Mock Trial Competition, giving an insight into the workings of the legal system, including the role of jurors.

www.cjsonline.gov.uk/juror/ – Information from the criminal justice system on jury service.

Think about your career

From the age of 14 years some students will have part-time jobs, but while still at school most students will not have the opportunity to take action for change through their work. However, they will start preparing for the world of work, and considering different careers. Most schools have a careers service and a work experience scheme to get students thinking about what they would like to do. One factor they can be encouraged to consider is how much potential they will have in future jobs to make a difference on the issues that concern them.

Some people work directly and practically to help individuals. Doctors, nurses, social workers and teachers can immediately see the positive impact they can have on the lives of those in their care. Those working for charities, whether as fund-raisers, managers or directly implementing the work of the charity, are responsible for the positive impact it makes.

Others work to make things better for everyone, to improve the conditions under which society operates. This includes politicians who make laws, lobbyists who influence them and lawyers who interpret them when they are made. Civil servants, from those working in government departments in Whitehall to those in your local council, ensure that decisions made by the government are effectively implemented. Scientists and other researchers work on technologies that can improve the quality of people's lives or even change the world we live in.

Across the private and public sectors there are opportunities for employees to make a difference to people and the environment, locally and globally. By considering the implications of their choices now, students will maximize their ability to make a difference in the future.

Find out more

www.ethicalcareersguide.co.uk – ethicalcareers.org is a careers service offering advice on how to forge an ethical career. It includes the experiences and ideas of people working in a wide range of ethical jobs, and a virtual ethical careers fair, which lists currently available 'real' ethical jobs.

www.oxfam.org.uk/generationwhy – This Oxfam website has a section on ethical careers.

6

Donate – money, time and things you don't need

Making a donation is an action for change that is completely age indiscriminate. Students may be low on cash, but they have time, creativity and enthusiasm, and their giving can be valued as highly as anyone else's. There are 170,000 registered charities in the UK, and all of them rely, at least in part, on donations from the general public to do the work they do. Help students to consider which charities make changes they think need making (see 'How can I decide where to donate?', p. 102), and how they can help their chosen cause. In general, students will not be able to carry out these change actions in lesson time, but they will benefit from time and support in exploring their options and planning their action.

Donate money

What opportunities can students think of to give money to charity? What about school events or religious services where money is collected? Have they ever been sent a letter asking for money, or donated their foreign currency on a plane? They may have sponsored a friend or relative to complete a challenge for charity, or seen a collection box in a shop. How many students have or would be happy to give money to someone who approached them in the street with a collecting tin? Remind students that it is worth checking that they have an ID badge and that collecting buckets or tins are sealed – official collectors have to do this to ensure that no one except the intended charity will benefit. Have students been to a charity event, like a dinner or concert, where they paid the entrance, but got an evening of entertainment as well as making a donation?

Ask students what they would do if they really wanted to donate to a specific charity, but could not find relevant collecting tins or charity events. Point out that it is possible to make a donation directly to any

How can I decide where to donate?

You may have direct experience of the charity you want to donate to. Perhaps you have benefited from their work, or seen them in action and think they are doing a really good job. Or you may have an issue in mind but not know which charity to choose. Either way it can be worth taking time to do some research. You want to know that the charity you give to is using your donation in a way that you are happy with.

The first step is to check if the charity is registered with the Charity Commission. This is a body that works to ensure that all registered charities fulfil their objectives and keep clear financial records. If an organization is not registered then they cannot call themselves a charity, and to get that status you have to be working for the 'public benefit' with clear gains for those groups you claim to help. Interestingly, this means that organizations that have lobbying as their main aim (such as Greenpeace), are not registered charities.

The nearly 170,000 charities registered in the UK all have different focuses. To find out more about the specific work a charity does, start by looking on its website. Do they work in places and on issues you want them to? Generally you cannot donate to one element of a charity's work, so are you happy with everything they do? Do you think they are having a positive impact? It is also worth reading what they say about themselves and their aims and ideals (try the 'About us' section of the website). Some charities are strongly religious, and you may or may not feel comfortable with their beliefs.

The Charity Commission's website, Guidestar UK, and CharitiesDirect.com all have searchable databases where you can find out the underlying objectives of each charity and the geographical areas they work in. You can search by charity name, but also by aims or issue, to help you narrow your search. CharitiesDirect.com and Guidestar can also give information on the finances of a charity, including the way that they spend their money.

Different people have different criteria that are important to them when they donate. Here are four issues that you might want to consider:

◆ **How much money does the charity spend on administration and fund-raising?** For some people it is extremely important that every penny of their money goes directly to help the problem it was intended for. Others are happy that the charity they donate to will spend a small proportion on running the organization, on fund-raising so they can do more work and in raising the profile of the charity. They believe that charities must be allowed to do this to sustain the work that they do and to be able to respond to unforeseen crises. CharitiesDirect.com can tell you how much the Top 500 UK charities spend on administration and fund-raising as a percentage of their total income.

◆ **Should I sponsor a child?** One way of donating that some charities offer is sponsoring a child in a poor country. You make regular donations and in return receive details of, and even letters from, the child you sponsor. Those who promote child sponsorship say that it allows the donor to see how the donation is used and gives a 'face' to the complex issues of development. It also enables the charity to work directly with families. Those against child sponsorship point to the money that has to be spent on the information and letters sent. They say that reminding such children of their dependence on a stranger, and giving glimpses of a different life, may cause dissatisfaction. Some claim that child sponsorship sets up tensions within the community between children that are sponsored and children that are not. Also, while the money you donate buys food, clothes and other practical items, it does not always tackle underlying issues such as disease and lack of clean water. To combat this, many child sponsorship schemes pool the money and spend it on projects to

(Continued)

How can I decide where to donate?—Cont'd

support the whole community rather than it going directly to a single family. Different sponsorship programmes work in different ways, and it is worth finding out more before you sign up.

◆ **Should I give to people who beg on the street?** Some people believe that it is sad if we cannot, as individuals, respond to pleas by other individuals in distress. Other people state that, like unregistered charities, people who beg are unaccountable – you do not know how they will spend the money they receive. Some say that it is better to donate to a charity that works with homeless people since you then know how your money will be spent. Such projects also work to get people off the streets and back on their feet, rather than continuing to rely on begging. An alternative is to buy a *Big Issue* magazine from a homeless vendor. The aim is to provide a business solution to a social problem: the vendors buy the magazines they sell, and in doing so gain the skills to make a legal living and improve their lives.

◆ **Should I donate my old clothes to an organization which will sell them in developing countries?** Textile banks, often found at recycling points, are generally not owned by charities, even if they have the name of a charity on them. They are owned by companies, called rag traders, who operate the bank and make a donation to the named charity. These companies also collect surplus clothes from some charity shops (ask your charity shop if this is the case). The clothes are used in different ways, but one way is selling them on to companies in developing countries, who in turn sell them on to other traders and, eventually, individuals. Some people say that clothes imported like this are causing local industries to decline, and that it is wrong to sell what is intended as aid, for a profit. Others say that it is unrealistic to give the clothes away because of the cost of sorting, packing and shipping. These businesses generate jobs and help the local economy, as well as providing clothes people can afford.

Find out more

www.bigissue.com – The website of the *Big Issue* magazine, written by professional journalists and sold on the streets by homeless vendors. Services that support vendors to overcome homelessness are provided by The Big Issue Foundation, the charitable arm of the magazine.

www.charitiesdirect.com – CharitiesDirect.com has comprehensive financial information about charities and a database of charity advisors.

www.charitycommission.org.uk – The website of the Charity Commission, the body that regulates charities.

www.guidestar.org.uk – Uses data from the Charity Commission to provide information on charities.

www.plan-uk.org , www.worldvision.org.uk – Two charities that work to improve the lives of children living in poverty. They raise some of their funds through child sponsorship.

www.shelter.org.uk – Shelter is a charity that works with homeless and badly housed people in the UK.

charity through a bank account (see details on bank accounts in the section 'Raise money for charity', p. 106). The website of the charity will be able to provide details on where to send a cheque, and may have a webpage through which it is possible to make online donations.

Students are unlikely to be in a position to set up a direct debit to a charity – but ask them why they think charities prefer to receive money like this, on a reliable monthly basis. Students may come across the term 'Gift Aid' and want to know what it means. Once they have a job and pay tax, they can tick this box when they make a donation and the government will give the charity 28 p. for every pound they donate (the charity gets the money that would normally be taxed from the donation, as well as the full donation).

Find out more

www.coinstar.co.uk – Coinstar is a company that installs coin machines in supermarkets. You can put all your small change into the machine, and it will give you either a voucher to spend in the supermarket, or the option to donate to a number of charities. Put your postcode into the 'search box' on the website to see if there is one near you.

www.ebay.co.uk – If you sell items on eBay™, you can donate part of your profit to charity. Click on the charity box when you are listing your item, choose the percentage of the final sale price you want to donate (10–100 per cent) and then select from the listed charities.

www.oxfam.org.uk/what_you_can_do/oxjam/index.php – Oxjam, an example of a music festival that raises both funds and awareness.

www.paypal.com – You can donate online or just by sending a text if you set up a Paypal™ account.

Donate on someone else's behalf

Have any of your students been given a donkey, toilet or beehive? There are an increasing number of websites that allow you to make a donation to charity on behalf of someone else; in a way that recognizes it as a gift for a friend or family member. Rather than just telling the recipient that a donation has been made on their behalf, the recipient often receives an e-card or card through the post telling them what has been donated. Students might enjoy looking at the range of gifts available: from a goat for a poor family, to protection for a penguin, to translating a book into Braille. Encourage students to check on the website how their money will be spent. Will it always be used on the item they choose? Does the organization allow flexibility to respond to local needs?

Find out more

www.goodgifts.org – There are lots of gifts at Good Gifts, helping a range of different charities.

www.oxfamunwrapped.com – Through Oxfam Unwrapped you can give gifts that help people work themselves out of poverty.

Raise money for charity

Fund-raising is the obvious way of enabling young people to make a larger charity donation than they can afford themselves. Students will probably have lots of ideas of their own. The most obvious is asking other people to donate to a chosen charity: to run a collection. While friends and family may agree to this, students should be aware that they need a licence from the local authority to collect funds on the street, in a public place or house-to-house. It is illegal to collect money without that licence, and even with it there are lots of additional rules to comply to. If students want to collect money on private property, like in a pub or supermarket, they will need to ensure they get permission from the owner.

So, it is generally a better idea, and more fun, for students to organize a fund-raising event or activity. Some basic strategies are outlined below, but students can find more creative ideas on the Giving Nation website. It is also worth encouraging students to contact the charity they want to donate to; they may be able to offer ideas and support. As specialists on fund-raising and the law, they will also know if a proposed event needs to follow any safety regulations, or will need any kind of licence, for example, for selling alcohol.

First, students could organize their own event, such as a concert, art exhibition or party, and charge people for entrance. For more ideas, see the change action 'Organize an event', in Chapter 3. Another way students can raise funds is to get themselves sponsored to do something. Many charities run challenges that individuals can take part in, or they can organize their own sponsored walk, football tournament or silence. Teachers can support students by making sure that they leave enough time to get sponsorship beforehand, and that they ask for permission to use the land, facilities or lesson time they need. Have they got a system for demonstrating to their sponsors that they completed the challenge? A third money-raising strategy is for students to provide a service, for which they charge. Examples include a bake sale, shoe shining or car-cleaning service.

Once people have given them money believing it is going to a particular charity, students are under legal obligation to get the money to the charity, preferably within four weeks of collection. Encourage students to count the money they make with other people present, and to keep a written record of what they have. Most charities do not have collection points for cash, so unless it is a few pounds that can go in a collection tin, students will have to make a bank transfer or send a cheque.

Most banks allow young people to set up a normal bank account once they are 18 years of age (sometimes younger if they have a steady income or an adult who will act as a guarantor). A basic or start-up account may be available for younger people, though it may not come with a cheque book or debit card. If they are raising a lot of money, students may be able to set up a bank account specifically for this cause. They will need to find out what services different banks can provide for them. If this is not possible or appropriate, students will need to ask a teacher or parent to make the payment for them, taking the cash and writing a cheque or making a bank transfer.

If students need cash or equipment to get their fund-raising event going, they can apply to a trust or approach a company for sponsorship. It is particularly worth thinking about local companies that may benefit from the publicity of being involved with a good cause. A business might agree to make a donation directly to a charity, give some money to help buy equipment needed to set up an event (e.g. bibs for a sponsored football tournament) or directly give something needed for the event (e.g. a printing company might print advertising flyers for free). Help students focus on what they need, and who they think might be persuaded to provide it. When contacting the chosen companies they might find the letter writing pointers on p. 80 helpful. In their letter they will need to explain who they are, what they are doing (including places and dates), what they are raising the money for and why, what they are asking the company to do and what the business will get out of helping them. They could offer something to the company in return, such as including their logo on publicity material.

To get students into the swing of donating, or as a quick and easy change action, have a look at the opportunities for giving on the internet. Students can use everyclick™ as their search engine. Every time they search the internet 1 pence will be given to a charity of their choice. Other ideas include TheGivingMachine™ (buy through this online shopping portal and a charity donation will be made for every sale), and 'ippimail' (a free email account provider that donates 55 per cent of the money they raise through advertising to charity).

Find out more

www.everyclick.com – Use everyclick™ as your search engine, and every time you make a search, 1 pence will be donated to your chosen charity, with no charge to you or the charity.

www.g-nation.co.uk – Website for young people with lots of ideas for fund-raising (have a look at the A to Z of fund-raising) and charity days and events.

www.institute-of-fundraising.org.uk – The Institute of Fundraising offers support and advice to fund-raisers.

www.ippimail.com – Register for an email with ippimail, who give 55 per cent of the money they raise through advertising to charity.

www.justgiving.com/process/raisemoney/ – Allows you to create a webpage about your sponsored activity so that people can sponsor you online, and then transfers the money directly to the charity of your choice. They charge a small transaction fee.

www.raceforlife.org – A sponsored run for Cancer Research UK.

www.thegivingmachine.co.uk – Register with TheGivingMachine™, and then every time you use it to order online from a big range of shops, the shop donates to your chosen charity.

Set up your own charity

If you have a committed group of fund-raisers among your students, who are unable to find a charity that does what they think needs doing, you could let them know that they could set up their own charity. Most charities start with someone caring so much about a problem that they decide to do something about it. They will need a lot of time and determination, as well as a clear rationale and plan, and adult help. The website of the Charity Commission, the body that regulates charities, is the best place to start.

Find out more

www.charitycommission.org.uk – The website of the Charity Commission.

Figure 6.1 *Name*: Tiphaine Deletraz.
What I think needs changing: Endangered animals going extinct.
The change action I took: Organized and advertised a bake sale for the WWF.

Volunteer your time

One resource that some students have plenty of, and which costs them nothing, is time. There is no age limit on volunteering (although there may be some limits on what young people can do, for insurance reasons). Many charities rely on volunteers to support and develop their work. It is also possible to volunteer for national and international bodies that are not charities, for example, as an intern at the European Parliament or the United Nations.

What do students think the benefits of volunteering are for the volunteer and the organization? Have they thought about what they could offer to a charity? Volunteers not only bring enthusiasm and energy, but can also bring skills to a team that are missing (e.g. computer know-how, or artistic flair). Volunteering is good for the volunteer too. Students could learn new skills, meet new people, grow in confidence and gain experience of a particular type of job or organization. For those starting to prepare application forms and CVs, demonstrating the commitment needed for volunteering looks good.

There are a number of websites that help match volunteers and charities (see the 'Find out more' section). If a student has a clear idea of which charity they want to donate their time to, they can approach the charity's volunteer coordinator directly. Before they approach an organization, students should think about what time and skills they have to offer. They also need to consider what kind of tasks they would be happy to do and what skills they would like to develop. Would they like to work at head office supporting administration, or would they prefer to be directly involved in the charity's work locally, for example, helping an elderly person with their shopping, or giving English lessons to people recently arrived in the UK?

Encourage students to reflect on the process of volunteering. What skills have they developed? What have they learnt? Do they feel that they have made a difference through donating their time?

Find out more

www.csv.org.uk – Community Service Volunteers is the UK's largest volunteering and training organization.
www.do-it.org.uk – A huge searchable database of volunteer opportunities.

www.timebank.org.uk – TimeBank is a national charity that helps match volunteers to charities.

www.vinspired.com – A volunteering site for 16–25 year olds with lots of advice and volunteering opportunities.

www.volunteering.org.uk – Volunteer England is an organization that works to support an increase in the quality, quantity, impact and accessibility of volunteering throughout England. They have got lots of advice on finding the right volunteer post.

Donate things that you don't need

There are many used items that it is possible for charities to make use of by reselling them to the public or to other companies. Not only does this raise some money for the charity, but it also prevents the items ending up in landfill sites, where they take up space and may even release harmful chemicals as they break down (see Chapter 2, section 'Reuse and recycle').

What items have students given to charity before? Is there anything listed in this section that they did not know they could donate? Books, clothes, toys, games, computer games, household items, CDs and DVDs are obvious charity-shop goods. Remind students that their donations should be in good condition, still work and be clean. They might not know that some charity shops specialize in books or clothes, and others have experience of reselling high value items like stamps or coin collections.

Do students know where and how to make their donations? The website of the Association of Charity Shops allows you to search for charity shops in the local area. Students may also have seen bags from charity shops delivered through the post box.

Charity shops can only sell electrical items if they can test them first for safety reasons, so not all shops can take things like kettles and DVD players – it is worth students checking first. However, many charities do collect electrical items such as old mobile phones and laptops. They don't resell these to the public, but to specialist partner companies who will revamp and resell them. The same can be done with empty ink and toner cartridges for printers. Charity shops and supermarkets are often collection points for these items, and some charities provide freepost envelopes to send phones or ink cartridges away in. Could students set up a collection point in school?

They could be involved in raising the profile of the scheme and encouraging their peers to donate their unwanted goods.

Find out more

www.charityshops.org.uk – The Association of Charity Shops website. Search by postcode for local charity shops.

www.recyclingrewards.co.uk – Schools and groups which recycle for ActionAid are sent a voucher in return, which can be redeemed through ActionAid for items like printer consumables, storage media, printers, fax machines and photo paper.

7 | Do something new . . .

This book gives an idea of the actions for change young people can take to make a difference, at home, school, locally, nationally or internationally. Through their practical actions, raising awareness, lobbying and donating, they can campaign on any issue or problem that they want to. As their teacher you can support them, in the classroom and beyond, by providing some answers to the question 'Miss, how can I make a difference?'

However, it is not possible to provide all the answers to this question. Some of the global problems we face, which could have a profound effect on what young people's futures are like, are unprecedented. The changes being made at the moment, including those in this book, may well turn out to be insufficient, or the wrong tools for change. New change actions may be needed.

Fortunately, with new technology, the actions available to those who want to bring about change are developing rapidly. 'Blogging' to raise awareness, online donations and email lobbying are all relatively new ways of making a difference. New practical actions and methods of lobbying will arrive all the time, and effective campaigns must adopt them.

Young people will be in a much better position to respond to these future challenges if they have already had experience of bringing about change. 'Real' opportunities for activism, which can come from the change actions in this book, develop the skills students need to participate effectively. This enables them to fulfil their right to a 'voice' on issues that affect them today. Not only that, but also, by gaining awareness of the world around them and their power to bring about change in it, young people will be better equipped to make a difference tomorrow.

More useful resources

Organizations, publications and websites supporting action for change

http://curriculum.qca.org.uk/subjects/index.aspx – The National Curriculum website. See the new Citizenship curriculum, implemented from September 2008.

www.changemakers.org.uk – Changemakers is an independent charity and social enterprise which enables young people aged 4–25 years to make a positive and continuing contribution to society.

www.citizenshipfoundation.org.uk – Youth ACT, a programme run by the Citizenship Foundation supporting groups of young people who want to achieve change in their school, youth club or community. The Citizenship Foundation have also produced:

Jarvis R and Thorpe T (2006). *Inside Britain: A Guide to the UK Constitution.* Hodder Education, London.

Thorpe T, ed (2007). *Young Citizen's Passport, England and Wales: 12th Edition.* Hodder Education, London.

www.csv.org.uk – Community Service Volunteers (CSV) supports volunteers and works with schools to provide opportunities for young people to make a difference in their local communities.

www.dea.org.uk – The Development Education Association (DEA) is a national network of organizations that shares a commitment to development education.

www.dfid.gov.uk/pubs/files/rough-guide/better-world.pdf – Online version of: Wroe M and Doney M, *The Rough Guide to a Better World,* Rough Guides and DFID. A guide to making a difference on development issues.

www.eco-schools.org.uk – Register to be an Eco-school, an international group of schools working towards education for sustainable development and a better quality of life.

www.oxfam.org.uk/generationwhy/index.htm – Generation Why is a website from Oxfam with lots of ideas of how young people can make a difference on development issues.

www.pledgebank.com – PledgeBank allows users to set up pledges which other people can then sign up to, for example, 'I pledge to pick up and dispose of at least one piece of litter per day, but only if 20 other people will do the same.'

www.teachingcitizenship.org.uk – The website of the Association for Citizenship Teaching.

Resources for teaching some of the issues in this book

www.actionaid.org.uk/schoolsandyouth/getglobal/ – *Get Global!* A guide for teachers on how to facilitate and assess active global citizenship.

www.amnesty.org.uk – Teaching resources, a teachers' network and visiting speakers for teachers involved in human rights education.

www.citizen.org.uk – The Institute for Citizenship has produced a range of teaching materials, including the following free resources: *Speakout! on European Citizenship, Teacher Guide* (to accompany the website www.citizen.org.uk/speakout), *Net Benefit* (an interactive CD ROM focusing on the use of the internet from a consumer perspective), *Consuming Passions* (a teaching resource on consumer rights and responsibilities), *Economic Citizenship* (a range of lessons exploring the economy, business and personal finance), *Learning through Elections, Learning through Local Elections,* and *How London Is Run.*

www.explore.parliament.uk – eXplore Parliament is a website from the Parliamentary Education Unit about parliament and government.

www.globaldimension.org.uk – This website from DFID is a database of books, films, posters and websites with a global dimension.

www.jusbiz.org– Just Business provides information and activities about global and ethical issues for students and teachers of Business Studies and Economics.

www.oxfam.org.uk/coolplanet/kidsweb – Oxfam's website for students on global issues.

www.oxfam.org.uk/education – Teaching resources from Oxfam that bring the global dimension into the classroom, including free online lesson plans and the Oxfam catalogue of resources for schools.

www.redcross.org.uk – The British Red Cross produce educational resources that promote humanitarian values, human dignity and awareness of the laws of war.

Index

Page references in *italic* refer to examples of student work
Page references in **bold** refer to information found in 'boxes' in the text